Preparing Children for Success in Reading

A Multisensory Guide for Teachers and Parents

Based on the work of Beth H. Slingerland

Nancy Sanders Royal

YORK PRESS **Baltimore Maryland**

This work is dedicated to Beth H. Slingerland
and to the thousands of teachers, and children and their families
who have learned and developed successful reading and written language skills
as a result of her pioneering work in multisensory education;

and to my grandchildren, Audra, Heath, Cheyna, Victoria, and Vanessa;
and to my "extended family" grandchildren Bryce and Shelly,
who constantly inspire me with their inquisitive minds, joy of learning, and loving hearts.

This work could not have been completed without the support, guidance, and shared knowledge of many individuals. Each one, adding his or her portion of research knowledge, experience, and instructional suggestions, played important roles. I hope that the reader will give careful consideration to the many references provided in Section C. It is through our shared knowledge that we grow strong.

The primary acknowledgment goes to my mentor, Beth H. Slingerland. Her generous sharing of knowledge, inspiration, and motivation has been a big influence on my professional and personal life. I appreciate her trust in requesting that I continue her work and revise her book *Prerequisites for Beginning Reading*. This book is based upon her earlier work, which has been revised, enlarged, and updated to meet the needs of today's children.

The continued encouragement, support, and great editing skills of Carol Murray, my friend and Slingerland colleague, have been invaluable. Her knowledge of the subject matter as well as her passion for language has greatly improved this presentation. Thanks to Regen Murray, a Slingerland- and Orton-trained tutor, for her editorial suggestions. Thanks also to the Executive Director, Debra Jarvis, and the students at The Prentice School for the use of their pictures.

I am grateful to Marc Lerner, M.D., Clinical Professor of Pediatrics, at the University of California, Irvine, who provided critical knowledge and a constructive review of the discussion on children's neural development. The support provided by Robert Perelman, M.D., Director of Education of the American Academy of Pediatrics, in reviewing this work and sharing their material is greatly appreciated.

My dear friend, the late Genevieve Oliphant, Ph.D., provided much language instruction during our years of working together in San Diego. It has been very useful to me as I prepared the section on language development.

I am also indebted to Marty Aho, Dean Emeritus of the Slingerland Institute for Literacy, who offered encouragement and reviewed the text.

And last, but not least, special thanks go to Victoria Rose Royal (age 3) for sharing her wonderful pre-school library, her love of books, her eagerness to learn, and her delight in her developing language skills with her grandmother.

Through working together, we will continue to learn more about the mysteries of the brain, learning, and effective instruction. This knowledge will enable us to enhance the educational opportunities for all individuals.

CONTENTS

Beth H. Slingerland was first and foremost a teacher—a teacher of children, a teacher of teachers, and a teacher of educational leaders. Among the latter group is Nancy S. Royal, Ed.D., founding executive director of The Prentice School in Santa Ana, California. Dr. Royal has been a Teacher Education Director, board member and on the Faculty Senate of the Slingerland Institute for Literacy. Her experiences include being a classroom teacher; program founder and director for the Slingerland Magnet Program in the Chula Vista City School District, California; supervisor and consultant to both elementary and high school districts; university instructor; researcher; and educational consultant. Dr. Royal has spoken at many conferences for reading teachers, classroom teachers, speech and hearing specialists, psychologists, physicians, parents, and the general public.

In her *Preparing Children for Success in Reading: A Multisensory Guide for Teachers and Parents*, Dr. Royal has fulfilled Beth Slingerland's desire and specific request to Dr. Royal to carry on her work by revising and expanding Slingerland's *Training in Some PreRequisites for Beginning Reading*. She would be proud of what Dr. Royal has successfully accomplished, for *Preparing Children for Success in Reading: A Multisensory Guide for Teachers and Parents* not only reflects Slingerland's pioneering work and philosophy, but it incorporates the latest educational research and neurological findings that support the prescribed teaching techniques and practices for successful language development in young children. This comprehensive, well-organized guide teaches the prerequisites for the development of language skills—the building blocks for the foundation leading to academic success. It supports the importance of explicit instruction and sequential alphabetic-phonetic instruction with phonological and phonemic awareness training at its core. It also emphasizes the importance of multisensory instruction. It includes many easy-to-follow, practical games and exercises that children, teachers, and parents enjoy. Just by reviewing a few of them, one can quickly see why they are so beneficial for developing language in young children.

Preparing Children for Success in Reading: A Multisensory Guide for Teachers and Parents is a most important and helpful instructional guide for pre-school, kindergarten and primary teachers and parents.

Marty Aho, Dean Emeritus, The Slingerland Institute for Literacy
Carol Murray, Murray Educational Services, Lexia Institute

Beth Haskell Slingerland became aware of the need for early language development, including the alphabetic processes now referred to as phonological awareness, many years ago. She wrote her first book, *Training in Some PreRequisites for Beginning Reading*, in Honolulu while working with Anna Gillingham and Bessie Stillman. This first work used pictures prepared by her mother, Harriet Davies Haskell. As time went by, Slingerland revised and further developed this work, always including the most current information.

Prior to her death in 1989, Beth Slingerland asked me to again revise this work, giving special attention to the newest information on language and early neural development. Knowing that the revision could not be completed at that time due to other professional commitments, we spent several weekends working together planning this project. Unfortunately, my activities in co-founding and directing The Prentice School, a non-profit independent school for dyslexic children, in Santa Ana, California, delayed finalizing this revision.

Since returning to this project, I have had the opportunity to review the latest research on language and reading, including the work funded by the National Institute of Child Health and Human Development; Human Learning and Behavior Branch grants. It was no surprise to find that this current, independent research reinforced the validity of Slingerland's philosophy and instructional techniques. The information she presented is as timely now as it was then. Indeed, Strunk (1982), Director of Special Education, University of San Diego, was correct when he declared, "Beth Slingerland was 50 years ahead of her time, both in program development and in her teacher-training model."

Because her work is as valuable today as it was during her time, activities from her last revision of *Training in Some PreRequisites for Beginning Reading* (Slingerland 1967) are included in this revision. As she wished, I have added information on early language and neural development and many additional activities. This includes a large section with strategies for teaching pre-alphabetic phonological awareness and reading for comprehension and enjoyment.

It should be noted that all information in this book had its origins with Beth H. Slingerland, whether it be in her exact words or in basic concepts. She has played an important role in my life as well as in the lives of over 14,000 dedicated Slingerland-trained teachers and the millions of children who have been taught by the Slingerland Approach. She was my teacher, my mentor, and my friend. I am privileged to have been her student.

It is my hope, as it was Beth H. Slingerland's wish, that you will use this work as a model for helping your children acquire learning skills. Working together, we will be able to help children develop their language skills to their full potential.

This book may be used by teachers and parents independently, but has been especially prepared for use in the kindergarten and primary levels of the Slingerland Institute for Literacy's Teacher Education Programs. Specific Language Disability (SLD) specialists have also found many of these exercises useful in building the vital language foundation that is often missing in older students with dyslexia (SLD).

This book is most helpful if it is kept on your desk and referred to regularly while planning lessons, rather than being read and stored on a bookshelf.

Skim through the book, develop an understanding of the scope of the instruction, and try some of the activities. Read Section II to assist in understanding the value of spending time in this instruction. The activities are brief and planned to meet a young child's attention span. Clear instructions and relevant word lists are provided to assist the teacher, parent, or other caregiver in easily using these ideas. Then, keep the book handy and integrate the activities in your daily lessons.

Reading: A Language Activity

Reading—the key to countless opportunities! Developing the skills of reading and writing greatly enhances communication. Through the magic of the printed word we are able to learn about our world, to understand our culture, to live vicariously—traveling through time and space. We are able to transmit our thoughts and histories to others in written form, be they near or far. The ability of the masses to develop these written language skills has occurred during the last two hundred years. Prior to that time it was reserved for a select few. The widespread ability to use these written language tools has resulted in an explosion of knowledge and advancement in all areas of our lives.

Children who are able to acquire communication skills early are at a definite advantage: academically, emotionally, and socially. With command of their language skills, they are able to exert increased control over their own destinies. Conflicts and problems can be solved, futures planned, and goals pursued.

During their early years, children learn through interaction with their environment. Beginning at birth, they gather information by looking, listening, touching, smelling, and tasting as they interact socially with their small but expanding world. Before a child begins to speak, the caregiver "reads" the child's messages through observation and interpretation of the child's behaviors. The caregiver, in turn, communicates with the child through his or her own touch, sound, and behaviors. (See Section B, Chapters 1 and 2, on brain and language development). As children develop spoken language, communication skills increase dramatically. Communication develops beyond meeting immediate needs to learning about their world.

The preschool years are devoted to physical, mental, and emotional development. The store of knowledge developed by children prior to entering school and their ability to express that knowledge constitutes the foundation for successful school experiences. The preschool years are ripe with opportunities for developing strong foundations through experience, being read to, and discussion.

Upon entering school, children are confronted with many new challenges and opportunities. Now, they must learn how to link information symbolically with letters and numerals in order to read, write, spell, and do arithmetic. These are exciting and special milestones in the lives of children. They are especially anxious and excited as they begin a wonderful new adventure: the adventure of learning to read and write. Children expect to read and write within the first few days of school. Parents and teachers know that it will take longer. However, as adults, it is usually hard to remember the complexity of their own experiences in developing literacy skills. They often expect the child to read and write within the first year. Although the acquisition of written language skills may seem like a magical gift, learning is work. Literacy requires a strong language foundation, and for some, learning to read, write, and spell is very difficult.

Reading consists of attaching sound and meaning to little squiggly lines viewed on paper, in books, or on computer monitors. These squiggly lines cannot have meaning without a well-developed inner language. Inner language is developed through both hearing and using language. Oral language is the natural basis upon which reading must be developed. Children need a firm foundation of language readiness in order to be successful in their academic experiences.

Often, reading is thought to be primarily a visual or sight process. Being able to recognize and recall the names of groups of letters is a great asset for learning to read; however, visual recognition is not enough for reading success. In order to become successful readers, children must be able to understand the relationship between individual sounds and words. They must be able to distinguish similarities and differences in sounds, and to put into sequence the sounds as they synthesize or blend the sounds into words. These words must be associated with information stored in their memory of previously learned information in order to understand the thoughts of the author. To read orally, the auditory memory of how the synthesized words sound must be integrated with the kinesthetic-motor memory of the movements of our speech mechanisms in order to pronounce words aloud. These procedures require a number of skills, such as auditory discrimination, auditory sequencing, phonemic segmentation, and auditory recall, in addition to developing inner-language concepts and the kinesthetic-motor abilities for speech.

As teachers and parents, our task is to make a variety of age-appropriate learning experiences and stimulation available. This responsibility demands careful observation of individual children as well as general knowledge of child development. The type of stimulation provided will be instrumental in determining which material the brain retains, and those that will be lost in the "pruning" (apoptosis) process. (See Section B for information on neural and language development.)

Providing developmentally appropriate experiences enhances language-processing skills. These experiences assist in preparing children for their triumphant journey through the wondrous world of learning. That's what this book is all about! The games and exercises in this book stimulate and direct the development of auditory, visual, and kinesthetic learning modalities. Most learning tasks depend on the ability to combine or "integrate" these modalities simultaneously. Therefore, more than one learning modality process is combined within individual games. Games and exercises are presented in a format that can easily be used with one child or with a group. Activities are planned to provide a broad spectrum of language-learning skills needed by beginning readers.

Additionally, information is provided to assist the reader in a better understanding of language development. Because the development and the readiness to begin formal reading depends so much on the development and myelination of neural pathways, a brief discussion of this vital process is also provided in the chapter on neural development. This chapter also includes suggestions for stimulating the development of neural pathways based upon suggestions provided by the American Academy of Pediatrics. Resources for further study are provided within the references.

INTRODUCTION TO LANGUAGE DEVELOPMENT

BETH H. SLINGERLAND (1969)

During the first years of life, foundations for the understanding and use of language are laid. This is a necessary prerequisite to further learning through reading. During these first six or seven years the child is an egocentric being, occupied with self and immediate surroundings. An understanding of language and ability for oral self-expression serve his needs. There is a close relationship between auditory perception and concept controlled by the central nervous system (Wepman 1962). To be noted are the observations of Piaget (1955), who found that at about the age of six to seven, the time when children change to ethnocentric beings, looking outward from themselves, they usually become ready to read. At this same time, the central nervous system is prepared to perceive and associate graphic symbols with previous language learning.

A baby's first experience with language is by way of audition, soon to be associated with the kinesthetic "feel" carried over the motor path of the speech organs. Language, or oral symbolic speech—single words that convey concrete meanings and then the grouping of words into entities for ideas and concepts—as Dr. Orton (1934) expressed it, becomes the "handle" by which each individual can communicate with others. Intelligence is the "soil" in which the language function can be grown. A child's understanding and use of language plays a large part in determining how he is to relate to other human beings. The sound symbols associated with concrete meanings, ideas, and both present and past experiences, enable a forward progression within the limits of native intellectual capacities and environmental opportunities. With time and usage, the language to which there is exposure serves as a means of "output" for individual self-expression.

Meaningful language will be associated with what is seen as well as what is heard. Not until the age of six or seven is graphic symbol required of children. At that time it is usually assumed that children are ready to perceive, associate, and recall the printed symbol in association with concept, and the auditory and kinesthetic patterns already acquired during the first years. If the six or seven year old has a mental age of six and a half or older (the age generally accepted as desirable for "readiness"), is emotionally and socially well balanced, has attained the expected sensory and central nervous system developments, he can be considered ready for introduction to the complex process of reading with reasonable expectations for success. However, all areas of development in every child are not always equal and in ideal balance. Sensory defects, neurophysiological impairment (brain damage), and neurophysiological dysfunctioning (disability) can interfere with learning as can emotional complications or impoverished or neglected environmental backgrounds. Teachers of kindergarten and first grade face these problems and challenges every day of their work with children.

The understanding teacher becomes sensitive to differences, weaknesses, needs, impairments, and possible disabilities. She must plan and organize in order to place emphasis on the kinds of help groups of children require. This is an enormous task. Before reading is introduced, kindergarten and beginning first grade teachers need to bear in mind two important factors related to language needs. First, little children must learn to understand and use the language to which they are exposed. This must come from without themselves because they have none at all when born. Second, most children develop within themselves a very perfect functioning of the threefold language pattern (Gillingham date?). Auditory configurations of sequential sound symbols that comprise words, the sequential articulatory movement patterns felt in pronouncing words (and later by the hand in writing), and the configuration of sequential graphic symbols, all work simultaneously without conscious effort to form this language pattern. Uncountable messages are carried over modalities of "input" to the cortex of the brain where they go through a process of integration before they can become motor patterns to be used over modalities of "output" (Wepman date?). Before reading is introduced, the auditory-kinesthetic channels in association with what is seen prepare the way for the visual graphic symbols which will be needed for reading, writing, and spelling.

Katrina de Hirsch (1957) writes, ". . . anomia—word-finding difficulty—is a significant and often neglected cause of reading disabilities." Emphasis needs to be placed on helping children hear and say words in association with objects and concepts. For all people, children or adults, a "heard" word must automatically be associated with an object or concept to be meaningful. Oral expression depends on deferred recall of names of words that express thought. When there is weakness, the child may perceive sequential sounds that make "whole" words so slowly that concept is lost or delayed. Directions are missed entirely or misunderstood, so performance is inadequate. Some have difficulty repeating a story or direction, or putting into words what they want to say. Some children require special help with organizing thoughts into sequential patterns associated with well-constructed phrases and sentences that are grammatically correct, while others require the opportunity for practice. For some, auditory perception and recall may not be as much a weakness as the kinesthetic-motor recall of the "feel" of the word or words in the speech organs. This, too, interferes with fluent speech. Words may be mispronounced. Whichever way, when words are not recalled, speech is blocked and communication lost. Too often the child is considered dull or shy, whereas step-by-step structuring of word with concept and opportunity to repeat orally, to put words together in sentences for self-expression with the help of the understanding teacher, can prevent or minimize these weaknesses. As far back as 1927, Judd stated, "Oral language is the natural basis upon which the reading of beginners must be developed. . . ."

For children with strong auditory-kinesthetic modalities and fluent speech, the games and exercises that follow give opportunity for enrichment. For those without this inherent, secure organization of the auditory and kinesthetic motor perceptions and recalls, the material provides suggestions for structuring and more specific guidance.

Prerequisites for Beginning Reading (pp. 1–3)

Section 1

Games and Exercises to Help You Help Children!

CHAPTER 1

Suggestions for Instruction

GAMES AND EXERCISES

All of this material is presented as suggestions for guidance to enrich, foster readiness, or give specific practice to children with different degrees of readiness in various language areas. These games and exercises are not meant to bypass the regular steps in child development or to rush children into formal reading.

"Centuries before human beings made any attempt to represent words by written symbols they were expressing ideas in spoken words. They learned, experienced, and enjoyed real things. In our modern pressure toward speed it is all too common to introduce little children to the printed word before they have experienced the actuality for which the word stands." Emphatically expressed, these words spoken by Anna Gillingham (1955), convey her strong belief in an adequate preparation for understanding and use of language for every child before he is exposed to reading.

Reading readiness tests have been critically examined to note the abilities that the makers of these tests have accepted as prerequisite for successful beginning. Their decisions were, of course, made after careful checking of their tests against the successful and unsuccessful members of many first grade classes. The games and exercises were constructed in the hope that they might reasonably be expected to afford training fundamental for these abilities. Comprehension and response to spoken words, i.e., following directions, are requirements of all standard readiness tests. The response, however, is not in language, but in brief acts:

"Draw a line through the picture that . . ."

"Draw a line showing the shortest path between . . ."

An attentive observer sitting quietly in a kindergarten or first grade classroom will be startled to note how extremely little real talking is done by the children in correct, full sentences. Affirmative or negative monosyllables, phrases, or short sentences constitute the bulk of children's language use during a school day. A grunt is often the only response.

When children begin to read from a book, they are expected to recognize a sentence and point out the terminal punctuation. Unfortunately, at this point in their lives, many children often have no real knowledge about spoken sentences. The exercises and games in the following chapters afford opportunity for practice in comparison, discrimination of differences and similarities and other such exercises, with responses expressed in clearly enunciated words and correctly constructed sentences. Often the best medium for the development of speech is guided discussion. In such discussion not only can vocabulary be enriched, but also many startling misconceptions of common names and processes are revealed and can be set right. For some children, this may mean willingness and even pleasure in speaking before a group or class. For others, being confined to one subject under discussion is difficult, and you will need to provide support and guidance in sticking to the subject.

At times, most children will need help with expressing their ideas in clear and explicit English. When the directed game experiences begin to carry over into spontaneous situations, one can be sure that progress is being made.

ARRANGEMENTS FOR WORKING WITH SMALL GROUPS

Some classrooms have assistants so that the classroom teacher can be free to work with small groups. Other classes use parent volunteer help. Parents selected to help usually give one or two hours a week. This frees the teacher for special group work. Whether working with paid assistants or parent volunteers, it is important for you to plan activities carefully and provide these wonderful assistants with clear directions.

GROUPING CHILDREN

The games or exercises, for obvious reasons, are useless with large groups. Children do not have enough opportunity for individual participation or for your undivided attention unless the groups are small. No more than eight to ten children can be effectively observed at one time.

There is generally a fairly wide span of maturity in any primary classroom. You should be cognizant of these differences and arrange to work with small groups of children with similar maturity. The less developed or younger children may need assistance, so their instructional period should be paced and geared to their attention span and specific needs without undue pressure or overshadowing by more developed and fluent children. During the day, they will overhear the language of those who are able to express themselves without difficulty and often colorfully. The individualized help given to them may improve their comprehension so the language of their companions takes on new meaning. For the more mature children with well-developing speech patterns, this period offers opportunity for enrichment and more advanced understanding and use of language.

Grouping will be especially important when teaching Phonemic Awareness. Lieberman's (1985) research indicates that the ability to distinguish individual phonemes or speech sounds is at a higher developmental level than the ability to hear syllables. She found these differences at the following approximate ages.

Age	4	5	6
Syllables:	about 50%	50%	90%
Phonemes:	0%	17%	70%

Care should be taken to provide appropriate instruction to meet these individual developmental needs.

TIME ALLOTMENT

The time allotment for each group depends upon the needs of the children, the number of children within groups, and the teacher's skill in holding the children's interest. In the beginning, eight to ten minutes may be all the time that some young children can stay focused. Sometimes the period may even need to be shorter. Other children can sustain interest and attention for 15 to 20 minutes or even longer.

STRUCTURING INSTRUCTION

Discussion or group activity should be teacher-controlled. It must be remembered that some children will have difficulty learning or recalling the names of objects (anomia). You may have to name objects being seen or felt by the child many times on successive days for the child to repeat. You may need to initiate the first words of a sentence to get a child "started," with the child always repeating so the words are "felt" as well as heard.

When practice in sentence construction is needed, you can say, "We say it like this" (putting the words together correctly), "so you say it after me and I will help you if you need help." Have the child repeat. Be relaxed in the approach. In time the child will gain security in his attempts at self-expression or will seek assistance. When extreme or frequent difficulty persists in an older and otherwise developed kindergarten child, a referral should be made for a speech and language evaluation. A notation should also be included on the report to the first grade teacher. It could indicate the presence of a language disability. For some children, it could mean environmental or developmental lags.

You should always speak clearly and distinctly. Sometimes it is necessary to overemphasize the syllables, as in "children" when it is pronounced "chilen" or "childern." You should be conscious of your own enunciation. Check with a dictionary when in doubt about the pronunciation of a word.

As you work with your children, you will become aware of those who quickly develop a skill and are ready to move on and those who need further guidance and time for development. This is where the art of teaching is important. You must be constantly aware that you are teaching children of a given age, not merely teaching curriculum. Matching developmental and learning needs with appropriate stimulation and instruction is vital in helping each child develop to his or her own potential.

TECHNIQUES FOR PRESENTING BOOKS AND PICTURES

Whether reading a book, showing pictures, or leading a discussion, it is important for teachers to maintain frequent eye contact with the children. The key to this is to be well prepared and familiar with the material. As you read a story, it is helpful to be able to hold the book up for all to see. As each page is completed, the book or picture should be moved in a smooth arc from one side to the other to allow all to see the pictures clearly. You can establish a smooth rate of movement by silently counting to 20 as the book is moved. This allows children on all sides to see clearly without boredom.

You should read the book with expression, being careful to observe good phrasing. Remember that you are modeling the way to read for enjoyment. This is your opportunity to use that hidden dramatic ability.

SEQUENCING GAMES AND EXERCISES

There is no fixed order in which the games should be introduced, e.g., a game of drawing with eyes averted may be played before or after one of auditory memory, and any game may follow or be the basis for the developing receptive and expressive language exercises.

There are five series of games: one primarily for developing language concepts, oral expression, phonemic awareness, and language organization. Three for sensory recall: visual, auditory, and kinesthetic, although in playing each of the sensory recall games one must keep in mind correct English usage. The fifth group of games pertains to left to right orientation.

The items in each of these series must be introduced in correct sequence, otherwise, preparation for the new game will be inadequate. For example, More About Classification on page 13 cannot be played satisfactorily until Vocabulary—Card Games on page 13 has become familiar; Noticing Change of Sequence in Groups of Objects on page 100 should precede Group Naming on page 100 etc. However, it is not only possible but highly desirable to have all five series progressing at once, e.g., the day after Describing Matching Objects and Pictures on page 12 has been played, Listening and Describing Environmental Sounds (object level) or Identification of an Object by Feel should be played. This can be followed a few days later by Visual—Kinesthetic Association—Bodily Movements. The only condition is that the sequence of the items in each series be in correct order.

It is desirable to repeat some games and exercises, but different pictures should be used where they are called for. The small cards can be used again and again, as can the pictures for classification. Otherwise, if this parallel introduction is not employed and the time allotted to these games is brief, it might be possible to end the school term with only the Listening and Auditory Based Activities to Develop Language Concepts exercises, but no sensory memory training accomplished. This would be an absurd negation of intent.

Instructions for making the folders mentioned in this section may be found starting on page 139.

CHAPTER 2

Language! Language! Language!

LISTENING AND AUDITORY-BASED ACTIVITIES TO DEVELOP LANGUAGE CONCEPTS

In the hearing population, language is mainly developed through the auditory modality or through information that we hear and process. There are a number of different auditory subskills. It should be kept in mind that children can exhibit both strengths and weaknesses in these various subskills.

Auditory skills include the ability:

- to attend to various sounds or words,
- to discriminate between various sounds or words,
- to be aware of their rhythmic and sequential patterns,
- to remember these sounds or words,
- to relate the sounds or words to concepts (past learned information),
- to organize these items in a meaningful way that will aid recall,
- to retrieve items from memory on demand,
- to organize and sequence retrieved items,
- to recall sounds and pronunciations for speaking, and
- to express these items through integration with the kinesthetic-motor activities of speaking, writing, or actions.

Success in these skills is dependent on a strong language base. The following activities will assist in developing these language concepts.

Vocabulary

FOLDER 1 Pictures to build vocabulary

Place one of the pictures before the children and discuss it with them. Name the objects in the picture, point out their uses, etc. In discussing a picture of people, encourage the children to observe such things as what the people are doing, where they may be going, how many there are, and whether they are grownups or children. Through such discussion in small groups, new words are introduced, the meaning of others clarified, general information enriched, and encouragement and individual help given for self-expression.

It is often useful for even young children to be familiar with the names of plane geometric figures such as squares, circles, triangles, and rectangles (see Naming Objects in Sequential Order from Memory on page 100). You can draw them on the blackboard, or use the geometric figures from FOLDER 20 in any other way that you see fit. For example, children can find objects around the room that illustrate these shapes. "The clock is a circle." "The door is a rectangle." "This table is a square." "That table is a rectangle." "This musical instrument is a triangle."

Describing Matching Objects and Pictures

FOLDER 2 Matching pictures
BOX 2 Duplicate sets of small objects or toys

Place three or four different pictures or objects in a row. To one side and clearly apart, place a picture or an object just like one of the pictures or one of the objects in the row.

A child takes one picture or object and matches it with one that is like it in the row of pictures or objects. He says, "This picture is like that picture" or "These pictures are alike (or the same)." If a child is unable to speak in a complete sentence, give him help, letting him repeat after you if necessary.

At this point, ask the child why he believes these pictures are alike. "The triangles are both orange." "The black and white dog is running after the boy." This assists children in noting and describing the details of the pictures (a skill that precedes the much more complicated task of Two Aspects of the Same Idea on page 22).

A variation of the above, after the children have had experience with some of the Chapter 3, Visual Processing and Recall games, would be as follows: This time, hold the picture or object and allow all to see it. Then remove it. A child finds the one just like you showed and says, "This picture of [names the object or toy] is just like the one you have." Then show the original picture again and the child matches his picture with that shown by you.

Vocabulary—Classification

FOLDERS 3, 4, 5, 6, 7, 8 Pictures for classification

Any one of the Folders 3, 4, 5, 6, 7, or 8 may be used. You are encouraged to constantly enlarge these collections.

Take several pictures from any one of these Folders and place them before the children. If you select the set from "Wild Animals," tell the children that all the pictures show wild animals. Discuss the term *wild animals* in contrast to *domestic animals*. The children learn the names of the animals as each one is discussed. This set of pictures could be used as a follow-up to a trip to the zoo, or it could be used in preparation for a visit to the zoo.

If you use the set of vegetable pictures, you could arrange a display of real vegetables in the room, or the children could bring pictures of vegetables to make a class chart.

Following the general discussion, say, "Show me a picture of a bear." After finding the right picture, the child responds, "This is a bear," or by using any other full sentence (with your help, if needed). Ask, "What kind of an animal is a bear?" The child answers with a statement: "A bear is a wild animal."

The contents of each of the Folders listed above are introduced in somewhat the same way. If you are using a picture of a lemon pie from the Food Folder, you may ask such leading questions as the following (helping to develop the answer if no child can reply, but being sure that the answer is in a complete sentence): What kind of pie is this? Why is it called lemon pie? (flavor) What else is in the pie? What is meringue? How is it made? What is the other part of the egg called? How is it used in this pie? How is it separated from the white? What is the crust made of? How is the pie cooked? When should the pie be eaten?

This affords an opportunity to help children pronounce words correctly, to use simple sentences, and to use their intellects.

Vocabulary—Card Game

FOLDER 9 Picture cards to build vocabulary and concept
Deal three or four cards to each child. Ask, "Who has a picture of a rowboat?"

The child with the correct card answers in complete sentences: "I have it. This is a rowboat."

As each card is named, it can be placed on the chalk tray or in the reading-chart holder or given to you. The first child to play all his cards is the winner. The other children may be given turns to name the pictures on their cards. The cards are again dealt. Taking turns, one child after another holds up a card, tells the others what picture is on it, and then places it in the reading-chart holder or on the chalk or white-board tray.

More About Classification

FOLDERS Any two of Folders 3, 4, 5, 6, 7, 8 may be used
After the children have had some experience with Vocabulary—Classification on page 12, place before them a few pictures from two Folders. In the first exposure, the contrast should be very great, e.g., Animals and Buildings rather than Wild and Domestic Animals.

> Teacher: "Someone show us a picture of an animal and tell us what it is." Choose a volunteer.
> Child: "This animal is a cow."
> Teacher: "Someone show us a picture of a building and tell us what it is."
> Child: "This building is a church" or "It is a church."

Continue in the same way with other pictures for the experience of naming what is seen. The child will hear and feel the word in association with what is seen.

In the beginning, some children may be able to do no more than name a word associated with a picture. The use of sentences will come later, after hearing you speak carefully in short sentences many times.

Some children should be given only one direction or question at a time until they can carry out a single direction successfully, e.g., "Someone show us a picture of a building." After the child does so, you can ask, "What building is it?"

Classification Card Game

FOLDER 9 Picture cards to build vocabulary and concept
Select and shuffle cards from three or four categories. Give several to each child. Say, "Show us pictures of something that makes music." All the children with cards belonging in this category stand before the other children holding their cards for all to see. Each child names what he has in his picture and places it in the reading-chart holder in a row with those of the other children. When a child needs help in naming, take time to give the help, being very sure to have the child repeat what you say. The child must feel what he hears in association with what he sees. The same procedure is repeated for each category, keeping each classification in a separate row. A child is a winner when all of his cards are gone.

Passing from left to right, point to each row of cards, helping children to recognize that, "All these cards have pictures of vegetables," or that the cards belong in whatever classification indicated.

A child who volunteers points to one of the rows of cards and says, "These are pictures of things to wear," or "These pictures show what we wear," or "They are all clothes."

Classification—Designated Category

FOLDER 9

Place a dozen or more cards in a row before the children. These should include cards from several classifications. Ask a child to find a picture of a <u>toy</u>, or <u>something to ride in or on</u>, or <u>a piece of furniture</u>.

The child begins at the left and points to each card until she reaches the correct one unless she sees it immediately. If she must search for it, insist upon the left-to-right progression. If recognition is immediate, there is no point in having her follow this routine. The child holds up the card, saying, "This top is a toy," or "This airplane is something to ride in," or "This chair is a piece of furniture."

This exercise is repeated with the different classifications.

Further Classification and Concept

FOLDERS Any two of Folders 3, 4, 5, 6, 7, or 8 may be used.

For example, <u>things to ride in or on</u> and <u>buildings</u> may be used. A child is given six or seven cards and asked to put together, in one place, all of the pictures of things to ride in or on. These should be placed in a spot that allows everyone to see. The child can make his selection from the two mixed sets.

When he finishes, he should begin at the left and name each picture in the order of his arrangement, saying, "_____, _____, _____, _____and _____ are all things to ride in." Help the children to understand that the selected set is to show only things to ride in or on. If a child should include a picture of a house, for example, ask, "Do we ride in a house?"

More Classification and Concept

FOLDER 6

Use pictures of food, empty clean cans, or play-food from the classroom playhouse or grocery store. Choose two or three categories, which may include fruits, vegetables, and dairy products.

Step 1. A child selects one item, places it in the correct grouping, and describes it to the group. "I have some beans. Beans are vegetables."

Step 2. A child selects five items, placing them in the correct groupings. The child then describes her purchases to the group, saying: "I went to the store and bought some groceries. I bought _____, _____ and _____. They are all fruit." "I bought ____ and _____. They are vegetables." (This is an excellent time to have meaningful counting and pre-addition exercises.)

Step 3. You may vary this exercise by asking the child to find a certain number of fruits and vegetables, etc.

Always end the exercise by having the children describe their categories.

Differentiation

FOLDERS Any one of Folders 3, 4, 5, 6, 7, or 8 may be used.
Several pictures are selected from one of these Folders, always with two pictures of the same subject treated differently.

Place in a row with other pictures the one that might have slices of white bread. Holding in your hand a picture that might have slices of raisin bread, say, "Find another picture of slices of bread." The child selects the right picture and says, "This is a picture of slices of bread."

The same sort of exercise can be developed using two pictures of the same category, which are treated differently from any of the other folders. Suggestions: two different airplanes, two dresses, two wagons, two cakes, two policemen.

Differentiation Developed Further

FOLDERS 3, 4, 5, 6, 7, 8, or 9
Take pictures from one folder. Somewhere among these pictures insert one picture from another folder. Ask the children which one does not belong in the row, and why. At first the differences should be quite obvious. After experience, the differences in classification can be subtler.

Suggestions:
buildings seen in a city / one farm building
foods we eat / one food we drink
farm animals / one wild animal
things in which we travel on land / one thing in which we travel in the air (airplane, hot air balloon)

It is possible that while the first parts of this exercise are entirely suitable for kindergarten, the subtler portions are better used in first grade.

Classification—Categories Common to Several Pictures

FOLDERS 3, 4, 5, 6, 7, or 8
On a reading chart holder, arrange two or three rows of pictures from different folders, e.g.:

house	church	barn
ship	train	bicycle
baker	doctor	grocery checker

Pointing to the first row, ask, "What one word tells about all these pictures?" A child says, "Buildings."

Then have the child name all the pictures, pointing from left to right and saying, "A house, a church, and a barn are all buildings."

Here is an opportunity to form groups to make little booklets or class charts using cutouts from old magazines and from pictures brought from home.

Categories can include clothes, dishes, cooking utensils, garden tools, furniture, toys, rooms of the house, animals, flowers, etc.

Contrasts and Resemblances in Complex Situations

FOLDER 10 Pictures for Contrasts and Resemblances

This exercise is essentially the same as Vocabulary on page 11, but presents opportunities for more advanced and abstract discussion.

Place three city pictures before the children. One child tells all he can in complete sentences about one of the three pictures (with help when needed). Other children in turn tell all they can about the other two pictures.

Then the group discusses all three of the pictures. In directing the discussion, you should bring out the salient points, getting each child to make full statements. You might bring out such points as the following:

"What do we see in big cities?" (tall buildings; narrow streets, sometimes very wide streets; cars, buses, and taxis; many people)

"When people want to look around, why do they go up in tall buildings?" (sometimes buildings get in the way when standing on the ground; too many people all around; it is fun to see things from a different angle)

"How do you move about in a city?" (walk on cement sidewalks and paved streets, ride in taxis, cross streets at certain places, obey traffic lights)

Show and discuss country pictures in the same way.

Next, compare and contrast life in the city and country:

"How do you know when you are in the country and not in the city?" (open fields, trees, only a few houses, barns, no tall buildings, not many people)

"How do we move about in the country?" (walk on dirt roads or paved roads, wander over fields or in woods, ride horseback or tractors as well as in automobiles)

"What are some of the things you can do in the country and not in the city?" (play in open fields, ride tractors, bring in cows, gather eggs, fish in streams)

Bring into the discussion what suburbs are and why people live there. What about the suburbs is like the city? (they both have places for people to live, people usually have more room around their houses in the suburbs, more people in the city live in large apartment buildings)

There can be similar discussions about summer and winter, day and night, land and sea pictures, etc.

Terms Needed to Develop Number Concepts

Select objects easily available in the classroom, e.g., blocks, dominoes, checkers, or colored sticks.

To aid in the use of terms needed in developing number concepts, use four or five dominoes and the same number or fewer of the blocks. Mix and place these before the children. Ask a child to arrange all the dominoes together and all the blocks together.

Help the children to see that they have arranged two groups, each with the same kind of objects. They should express this fact in words: "This group is all dominoes and this group is all blocks."

Then ask a child to find out how many dominoes are in one group. If he says there are five dominoes, ask, "How did you find out?" The meaning of counting to find how many may require some discussion and instruction at first. Next, ask the child to show how he counts by pointing to each domino, beginning at the left and moving to the right. When the counting is completed, the child rounds out the whole operation by saying, "I counted five dominoes in this group." He counts the blocks in the same way.

The meaning of more and less can be developed following experience with the exercise just described. For this exercise, two groups of like objects are provided, one larger than the other, e.g., five checkers and three checkers.

One child counts one group and another child counts the other group.

Teacher: "Which group has more?"
Possible response from child: "The group with five checkers has more."
Teacher: "Which group has less?"
Possible response: "The group with three checkers has less."

Later, help and encourage the children to say, "This group has more checkers than that group because five is more than three," or "This group has less checkers than that group because three is less than five."

Some children cannot be expected to say more than, "This group has more checkers." You will need to ask, "How can you tell?" Then the child may say, with help, "Five is more than three (three is less than five)."

Guessing from Descriptions

As the game begins, you describe and the children guess. Describe some animal, person (policeman, farmer, doctor), building, bird, tree, etc., so that the children can guess what it is. Encourage the children to say, "I think it is a robin," if this is the bird described. Encourage the child to tell why he thinks it is a robin. Perhaps the response would be: "Because you said it has a red breast."

If a tree has been described, the child might say, "It is an evergreen tree because you said it has needles instead of leaves."

A child may select some picture, not allowing the others to see it, and describe in sentences what she sees for the others to guess. The child may need help in expressing herself.

You may help her by saying, "What do you see here?" The child may respond with a run-on sentence. To assist the child in correcting a run-on sentence, say: "Now what is that?" "Say that, and stop." Again, "Tell the children what this is and stop." Thus you prepare the way for groups of words followed by periods, which the children will soon meet in their reading (sentences).

After the children have had much experience in describing pictures, they will be ready to progress to describing something without the aid of a picture. One child chooses another child to guess what he has described.

Prepositions—Relation Words

Place a box, a basket, or any other container before the children.

Say, "Put the pencil in the box" or ". . . on the box" or (after experience with Duplicating Sequence with Colored Blocks from Memory on page 113), "to the left of the box." The child responds by doing as directed and by telling where he or she placed the object, as "I put the pencil in the box."

To change the game a little, the child places the object himself and tells where he put it, using a complete sentence.

To develop the use and understanding of an interrogative sentence, a child places the object and asks another child where it is, using a complete interrogative sentence. The second child answers in a full sentence. She then places the object in a new place for the game to start again. Again, tell the child how to ask a question or make a statement when this help is needed.

Playing Hide the Thimble with Prepositions—Relation Words

The same idea may be brought out by the old-fashioned game "Hide the Thimble." Two children cover their eyes or turn their backs. A third child places a thimble or any small object within a given area where the other children can watch. The thimble should be placed in, on, over, under, etc. some part of school furniture or equipment.

When the thimble has been placed, the two children who are "it" look for the thimble. The first one to find it and tell in a full sentence where it was will be the one to hide it next.

Example: "I found the thimble on the teacher's desk."

Prepositional Phrases—Concept

FOLDER 11 Pictures that lend themselves to use of prepositional phrases
Place several pictures before the children and select one, saying, "The clock is <u>on the wall</u>. Where did I say the clock is?" A child is called upon and says it is <u>on the wall</u>. Tell the children "on the wall" is called a phrase. (By casually telling the children what a phrase is many times over a period of days or weeks, they come to understand the meaning.) Then ask a child to describe one of the pictures using a phrase such as the one the child just used.

The child holds up another picture and says, "This clock is <u>on the table</u>." If he is correct, he may choose the next child to have a turn. (Help the child call upon the next one by name, not pointing or calling him "you.")

Hold up a certain picture and say, "Here is a family. Tell <u>where</u> the family is, using a phrase." The child answers in a full sentence, "The family is <u>in the house</u>."

In this way various prepositions can be introduced, such as <u>in</u>, <u>out</u>, <u>up</u>, <u>down</u>, <u>inside</u>, <u>outside</u>, <u>across</u>, <u>through</u>, <u>from</u>, <u>toward</u>, <u>above</u>.

Before this exercise can become effective training in the prepositional phrase concept, you must accumulate a large collection of pictures. Often, the school book room or district library will have outdated books that provide a good source of pictures.

Playing "Hide the Thimble" to reinforce use of prepositions.

Prepositions Activity—Concept

FOLDER 20 Geometric plane figures plus 1 large button, 1 small button, and 1 large piece of construction paper per child.
This activity should be done with individuals or small groups (six or fewer) and follow Right and Left on page 112, Following Right and Left Directions—Stepping on page 114, and Pointing to Objects on the Right or Left on page 115.

Each child has a large piece of construction paper, a large button, and cutout shapes including a triangle, square, rectangle, and circle. (Children should have been taught names of shapes prior to beginning this game. This activity should follow Following Right and Left Directions—Stepping on page 114.)

Prior to beginning the game, review the shapes, asking children to hold up the square, circle, rectangle or square and triangle. Then direct the children to place the cutouts on the construction paper in a given left to right sequence. Next, they "read" the sequence (left to right): "I have a square, a ____, a ____, and a ___."

The next part of the game involves using the large and small buttons to develop the concepts <u>on</u>, <u>above</u>, <u>under</u>, and <u>beside</u>.

When the children are comfortable with these words, the concepts of left and right may be added.

A variation of this game is to play "Simon Says" using the concepts on, above, under, beside, left, and right. "Simon Says" is described in Pointing to Objects on the Right or Left on page 115.

Adjectives—Concept

FOLDER 12 Pictures that lend themselves to the use of adjectives.
The first two pictures used might be those of a young person and an old person and you might ask, "What is the difference between these two women (or men)?" The answer would be, "One is young and one is old." "What words describe the women?" "<u>Young</u> and <u>old</u>." To help with concept, ask the children what words <u>tell about</u> or <u>describe</u>.

For example, if a picture shows a child looking out at the rain, your questioning can bring forth such responses as a <u>cloudy</u> sky, a <u>rainy</u> day, a <u>sad</u> child, and a <u>disappointed</u> boy.

Singular and Plural—Concept

FOLDER 13 Pictures that lend themselves to the language of singular and plural with the concept of one or more than one
The purpose of this exercise is not only to develop the concept of singular and plural, but also to teach new vocabulary words. Its object is not merely to familiarize children with the idea of singular and plural but also to enable children to use readily the terms "singular" (<u>one</u>) and "plural" (<u>more than one</u>).

It is also a valuable exercise in articulation and auditory discrimination. Many upper grade children continue to have difficulty in distinguishing between singular and plural sounds, e.g., boy versus boys.

The exercise begins with a discussion of the meaning of singular and plural. Objects are used to illustrate that we say "book" when speaking about just one book and "books" when speaking about <u>more than one book</u>.

Ask a child to place before the group a certain object or objects depending upon your direction. "Show us what we mean if we say pencil," or "Show us what we mean if we say pencils." The children will soon learn to see and understand that we say "<u>pencils</u>" for any number of pencils that are <u>more than one</u>. This will be one more way in which to build the singular-plural concept and to use correct terminology to express the concept of: a pencil, this pencil, one pencil, some pencils, these pencils, several pencils, two, three, or four pencils, depending upon the number or article used before the noun <u>pencil</u>.

Following practice and experience with the above exercises, pictures can be used to illustrate singular versus plural. Say that you are going to show the class some pictures. Some will contain just one object and others will contain <u>more than one</u> of the same object. Together, they agree upon a place to arrange the pictures that will <u>tell about</u> just one and another place for the pictures that will <u>tell about</u> more than one.

Hold up a picture. A child puts it in one of the two pre-selected locations.

Help the child to say, "This is a picture of <u>one shirt</u>." If the picture illustrates the plural form, he says, "This is a picture of shirts." He might say "several <u>shirts</u>" or "some <u>shirts</u>."

Depending upon the maturity and language background of a particular group of children, such singular and plural forms as child and children, man and men, fireman and firemen, policeman and policemen, deer and deer, sheep and sheep can be introduced.

Picture Stories

FOLDER 14 Sets of pictures, each set intended to illustrate incidents in a story
Place one set of pictures in the correct sequence before the children. The children discuss the pictures and tell a story suggested by the set of pictures, possibly with some help.

After the details have become familiar to the children, the pictures are exposed in random sequence. One child after another places the pictures according to the sequence of events in the story. As each picture is selected, the child places the picture and is encouraged to tell that part of the story.

At another time, place the same set of pictures in the correct order but with the backs of the pictures facing the children, in left to right order. One child tells the first incident of the story from memory. The first picture is then exposed so all can see whether the child's incident and the picture correspond. If the child described the wrong incident, he is given the opportunity to describe the one in the picture. Then another child tells the next incident—the next picture is exposed, and so on. As a summation, if a child can relate the complete story, he or she may do so.

On another occasion, the pictures are placed before the children in order, except for one which is placed out of order. A child finds the picture that is incorrectly placed and puts it in its proper sequence. The child then says, "In the story, the _____ came after the _____."

More work with sequencing will be found in other parts of this book.

Child arranging pictures in sequential order.

Promotion of Thought by Pictures

FOLDER 15 Pictures to promote thought

Only one picture, or at most two, can profitably be used in one lesson.

The children discuss details of the picture with you. Example: If the children are looking at a picture of groceries being delivered, encourage thought with such questions as:

"Whom do you see in the picture?"

"What room are they in?"

"Why are they in this room?"

"Is the big boy part of the family?"

"What is the mother doing?"

"What is a list?"

"Can you name another kind of list?" (shopping, laundry, Christmas)

"What time of the year is it?"

"What gives us that idea?"

"Why are some things wrapped in transparent paper?" (give an explanation of <u>transparent</u> and plastic bags, if needed)

"From what kind of store do they come?"

"How do you suppose the delivery person knew what things to bring to the house?" (telephone, Internet, or a list left by father or mother on way to work)

"How do you get your groceries?"

If you are using a picture of a mother and girls having their photographs or pictures taken, encourage thought with such questions as:

"Why is the father taking the picture?"

"Where could they be going?" (church, wedding, party)

"What special day could it be?" (Easter, Christmas, Thanksgiving, Hanukkah, Kwanza)

"What are the little girls carrying?"

"For whom may the picture be taken?" (grandmother, aunt, friend)

Such discussion offers great opportunities to widen concepts and to increase receptive (received and understood) and expressive (spoken) vocabulary. It encourages thought based on observation and deduction.

Reproducing a Story

FOLDER 16 Pictures to use in reproducing a story

Tell or read one of the stories to the children, placing the corresponding pictures to illustrate the main events of the story as it is told.

Then rearrange the pictures out of order and let the children, one at a time, place the pictures according to the sequence of events in the story. Help each child state at least one sentence about the picture while placing it in the correct order.

Then encourage each child, or two or three children, to tell the whole story using the pictures to keep the events in order.

As an alternative, sometimes a child relates the story sitting with his back to the pictures and facing the group. The others listen and watch to see whether their classmate relates the events in correct order or omits a part or two.

It takes more than one period for this exercise. On one day, probably no more than the story would be read or told to the children. On the next day, you should lead the children in reviewing the story before children are expected to perform individually.

This is one of the exercises that also fits under the topic "sequencing."

TWO ASPECTS OF THE SAME IDEA

FOLDER 17 Pictures to give two aspects of the same idea
(Before attempting this exercise the children should have had experience with Adjectives—Concept on page 19.)

Separate the pairs of pictures giving the same idea or showing the same action into two sets, each set containing one picture of each pair. Keep one set and place the other before the children, who observe and briefly discuss the pictures.

Select one picture from your set and show it to the children. Lead some discussion about it, noting details and the general idea conveyed by the picture.

Then the children look at the other three or four pictures arranged before them. One child finds a picture that makes him think of the one you are holding—the one just discussed.

The children note why the two pictures give the same idea. The discussion should bring forth reasons why the two pictures convey similar meanings or ideas. Help them notice differences in detail while recognizing that two different artists have expressed the same idea.

If you are using pictures of little girls about to drink a beverage, the main idea that both little girls are about to take a drink is readily seen.

Similarities of detail:

Both are holding a glass.

Both are smiling.

Both are looking at us.

Both seem happy.

Differences in detail:

One has milk and the other has orange juice. (How do they know it is orange juice?)
Their dresses are different.
One has dark hair and the other has light hair.

You may ask questions to promote more subtle deductions: "Which little girl is older?" and "What makes you think so?" A child might answer: "One needs two hands to hold her glass and the other can use just one hand," and "She looks older, too" (aesthetic appreciation).

If you are using pictures that have families eating together, one at home, one on a picnic, the following points might be noted:

Both groups are having meals together.
Both groups are having fun.
One group is at home; the other group is in the mountains (beach, riverbank, yard).
One group is inside, one outside.
One group is eating with silverware.
The other group is using chopsticks.

Note differences in clothing, furniture, food, table settings, etc.
Also give attention to members of each family.

This exercise is intended for first grade rather than kindergarten children unless the kindergarten group is advanced.

Promotion of Thought by Word Association

FOLDER 18 Pictures of single objects
Place a picture of a single object (without background) before the children. Ask the name of the object.

Then ask the children to think of the names of other things or ideas that this word brings to mind. If a picture of a mother is shown, children might answer with words such as pretty, daddy, baby, love, home, or children.

You can help by asking thought-provoking questions, i.e., "What are some of the things that mother does for the family?" or "When you think about a lake, what else do you think about?"

After there is familiarity with this exercise, vary the procedure by making it into a game that, in turn, can be associated with counting.

One child names all the words he can associate with the picture. For each word named, put a cube or other "counter" object on the table. Other children may think of more words that can be counted. Then, all the cubes can be counted. To sum up the activity, a child says, "We thought of _____ words."

Two children, each with a different picture, can play while others watch.

One child names all the words his picture brings into his mind, a cube being placed to represent each word. Then the other child has a turn. The blocks are counted. Obviously the words must have a clear relationship with the picture word, or the game is without purpose. Emphasis is on words, not on cubes, which only stand for the words.

It is hoped such games will help when reading is introduced at a later time by encouraging children to think of words and ideas that might relate to what is being read.

Verbs—Present and Past Time Concept

Ask a child if he can run. The child probably answers in the affirmative. Tell a child he may run to a given point, but first he must tell what he can do.

Teacher: "Tell me the one word that tells what you can do."
Child: "Run."
Teacher: "Yes, let's see you run."

After the child performs as directed, ask the other children, "What did he do?"

Children: "He ran."
Teacher: "What can he do?"
Children: "He can run," or "Run."

Casually call attention to the way run and ran were used—how one word tells what you do right now and how the other word tells what you did. Other action words for performance to be associated with language are:

skip	kick
hop	hum
tap	push
pull	reach
clap	turn
step	lift

Verbs—Present Tense and Present Participles

After familiarity with Promotion of Thought by Word Association on page 23, follow the same procedures with present and present participle forms.

> Wave your hand and say, "Mary, if you do what I do, what <u>do</u> you <u>do</u>?"

> Child: "I <u>wave</u>."
> Teacher: "When Mary and I do this what are we <u>doing</u>?"
> Other children: "<u>Waving</u>."

> Do not spend time giving lengthy explanations.

Repeat the game with different action verbs that are easy for children to perform, always including practice with the associative language pattern, so concept will gradually become clear.

ACTIVITIES TO DEVELOP AUDITORY ATTENTION AND RECALL

Listening and Describing Environmental Sounds (object level)

These auditory exercises begin with a discussion of the importance of our ears and listening. Ask the children to tell some of the things they learn through their ears. They may close their eyes, be very quiet, and listen for some sound that may come to them from within or outside the room. Let them identify the sound and think what that particular sound may tell them—the clock, someone walking in the hall, children outside, a bird singing, a bell whose signal conveys some message, or an airplane.

Sometimes the children cover their eyes or put their heads down and you may tap on the wall, bounce a ball, tap a bell, or clap your hands. The children tell what the noise was and how many taps or bounces they heard.

Help children to answer in a sentence by asking, "What did you hear?" The answer is, "I heard a bell." Structure the sentence to be repeated by the child who cannot do it for himself.

> "How many rings did you hear?"
> "I heard two rings (or three, or four)."

Some can say, "I heard a bell ring two times." For others, the two concepts are more than they can express at one time.

Rhythms (object level)

Rhythm is also important in helping children learn to focus on sounds that they hear in the environment. Developmental experts tell us that we are rhythm bound organisms. It has been suggested that early exposure to rhythm assists in patterning and organization of the brain. Listening to music, singing, and rhythmic movements appear to support this development. Activities that pre-school, kindergarten, and primary school children enjoy and that will further develop the attention to and sense of rhythm are as follows:

Walking—Moving to the Beat
Children love to march and move to music. As you introduce these movements, it is helpful to use a recording for accompaniment. This allows you to be directly involved in the movement. As activities vary, you may play the tom-tom, piano, or other rhythm instrument to accent the beat.

The first experience should be relatively unstructured. Explain that they will be listening to the music and that it will tell them how to move their hands and feet. During the first playing of the music, you and the children should clap your hands to the music.

Marches are written in 4/4 time, which means that there are four beats to a measure and that they are all of equal length. Children will clap their hands on every beat as each foot touches the floor. Then, with you leading, the children should march to a recording or tape. As the march continues, you should lead the children in clapping their hands as they step.

The next activity also involves the children marching to the music; however, this time you will accompany them with a strong drum beat on the first of every four beats, just as the left foot touches the floor. (Don't worry too much if children are on the wrong foot. The point is to accent the first beat. Gradually, you will be able to work out the correct foot placement.) As children become used to marching to the 4/4 beat, select two or three children to play the drums (or tambourines) with you. Work with them to only play on the first beat.

On a later date, you will be able to add other rhythm instruments playing on the first and third beats. Still later, the rhythm sticks can be added to play every beat. Emphasis should be on listening to the music.

As children become accustomed to listening for the beat, movement can be done with only a drum accompaniment. Ask them to move in the circle as they listen for the drum beat. They will need to listen carefully, as sometimes the beat will change and the drum will tell them to move slowly, and sometimes it "says" to move quickly.

Rhythm Instruments and Moving Hands and Feet to the Beat

Now that the children have been introduced to listening to the beat of music, they are ready to accompany the piano or recording using more instruments.

Emphasis should always be on listening so that the music can guide their activity.

Different rhythms should be introduced. When introducing a new time pattern, it is useful to have the children clap to the music. Then instruments can be added.

Use of Listening and Movement Activity Records

A number of excellent listening and movement activity records are available at your local teacher supply store. "Hap Palmer," "Kids in Motion," "Rock 'N' Roll Fitness Fun," and "On The Move With Greg & Steve" are a few of these fun-filled activity records.

Echo Clapping

Explain that they are going to play another listening game. Ask the children to listen and then to clap the same rhythm that they heard you clap. The rhythm should be clapped as if counting music to 4/4 time (count of four beats to a measure).

After listening, the children clap the echo of this rhythm.

Be sure to keep the rhythm going in 4/4 time (march time).

Beat:	#1	#2	#3	#4
	long	long	short, short	long
	long	long	long	long
	long	short, short	long	short, short
	long	rest	long	rest
	short, short	rest	short, short	rest

Make up additional patterns.

Associating Taps to Written Patterns

Folder 23 Pattern cards made with large and small colored dot stickers plus rhythm sticks or un-sharpened pencils

Echo Tapping and Rhythm Sticks

When children have become familiar with echo clapping, they are ready to be introduced to tapping patterns using rhythm sticks.

Begin by having them do Echo Tapping, just as they did Echo Clapping. Explain that instead of clapping, they are going to learn to tap with the rhythm sticks.

After passing out sticks, talk about the sticks being instruments and have them put them quietly in their laps (or with arms crossed, put sticks in upright position in front of their chests) until they are ready to use them.

Ask the children to listen closely to the rhythm you tap.

Tap: <u>long, long, short, short, long</u>.

Children echo taps. Continue using patterns used in echo clapping. In the beginning, avoid using rests. When playing "rests" the children raise their sticks up and turn their wrists slightly outward.

Reading and Playing Rhythm Patterns

After several days of Echo Tapping, show children a pattern card (or draw one on white or chalk board). Demonstrate reading the pattern while tapping the rhythm.

Repeat this step several times.

Pass out rhythm sticks.

Place pattern card on card chart or on the board.

Lead children in playing this pattern.

Repeat this step with several patterns.

Give children opportunities to read and play one of the previously practiced patterns by themselves.

Associating Tapped Patterns to Written Patterns

On this day, the children are going to identify a pattern that they heard. Display two different pattern cards. Tap a rhythm. Have a child identify the card that depicts the rhythm.

A variation of this activity is to display two or three different pattern cards. Tap a pattern under the desk in a manner that is not visible to the children.

A child selects the correct pattern that has been depicted on a card.

Early Echo Speech (language level)

With younger or less expressive children, names of objects may not be recalled (anomia).[10] You can point to different objects in the room, on a person, in pictures, or outside, to be named by <u>a child</u>. If the child hesitates, pronounce the word, have the child repeat it, and then ask the group to repeat. Let the child choose the next child for a turn. The child should name, not point to, the child who is chosen.

Sometimes this same procedure should be followed by pointing to different children for their names to be learned.

More Echo Speech

This game should be preceded by practice in the simple, immediate echoing of a word or phrase spoken to a child by <u>you</u>, but not initiated by another child.

Whisper a word into a child's ear or, better, take the child behind a screen or outside the door, and utter it distinctly in a low tone.

The child repeats it softly to another child, who then says it aloud so distinctly that a child volunteering, or chosen from the group, can hear it clearly and repeat the word before explaining or using it in a sentence.

Not infrequently, the word is echoed so poorly as to be unrecognizable.

On the other hand, as the children become familiar with this exercise, they may be able to have the word pass through two or three intermediate children and still emerge as a clear and understandable word.

Words chosen for the Echo Games can progress from monosyllables to two or three syllables. It must be understood, however, that <u>all words used in this game are those that are well known</u> to the children.

Suggested words:

desk	table	February
floor	crayon	cafeteria
chalk	crayons	groceries
door	window	library
lamp	pencil	eleven
pencils	picture	pitcher
chimney	police	airport
pumpkin	party	invention

Echo Speech—Child Initiates the Stimulus Word

After a considerable period of experience with More Echo Speech on page 26, a child who has been outstandingly successful in catching and repeating a word may be called upon to initiate a word—first telling it to you—to be passed along a row of three or four children.

The children must be told to turn and repeat at once, one by one, what they think they heard. The turn is completed when, after passing the word from ear to mouth through several children, the word emerges as an inarticulate buzz.

Then, let another three or four children have a turn.

Echo Speech—Deferred Recall

The Echo exercises demand accurate discrimination and correct reproduction of speech sounds. They employ immediate recall, whereas correct speech and reading depend upon deferred recall. People differ greatly in their ability to recall a word heard in conversation or the pronunciation of a new or foreign word learned correctly a few days before. This is an inherent difference, but specific training, by riveting children's attention, can accomplish a good deal. Two or three children are taken aside separately, one by one, at the beginning of the period and given a word to repeat until correct pronunciation is attained. Each child is told to remember his or her word. Help children <u>associate their word with some idea or object</u>. Asking them to visualize how the object named by the word looks, or to think about what the word means may do this. Tell the children you will ask them to say the word to the group at the end of the period or at some other time in the day.

At the right time, in response to your question, "What was the word you were to remember?" each child names his or her word. If a child is unable to recall or to pronounce a word correctly, restate the word and have the child repeat it.

At times, if a child cannot recall a word, ask him to show what was to be named. Frequently, children understand or have the concept but are unable to recall the words needed in communication. This lets you know you must pronounce the word for the child again, and be sure the child repeats the word in order to <u>hear</u> and <u>feel</u> the word. The same word, associated with an object or idea, should be used until it can be recalled without hesitation.

Words chosen for this game should be familiar in meaning. If eagerness to reproduce long words has been built up, some of these may be used. Or the selected word may be one recently discussed or frequently mispronounced in the class or in the community. For example: <u>chimbley</u> for chimney, or <u>crick</u> for creek.

It may be that a child will unconsciously defeat the auditory purpose of the game by remembering the meaning rather than the correct pronunciation. For example, if you said "across," the next morning, the child may proudly repeat the word that he habitually uses for that meaning, "acrost." The child should be given another "try" at the same word. The period of deferment can gradually be lengthened to overnight or over a weekend.

Recalling a Series of Directions

This should not be used until after Prepositional Phrases—Concept on page 18.

A game of auditory memory, though somewhat different in intent, may be a single direction or a series of 2, 3, 4, or 5 directions.

For some, perhaps a single direction is all that can be carried out until auditory memory lengthens. Direct, "Walk to the bookcase." The child repeats the direction by saying, "Walk to the bookcase," or "You said to walk to the bookcase." Repeat your direction until the child can echo.

When two or more directions are given, emphasize each phrase, i.e., "<u>Put the pencil on my desk</u>." Suggested directions:

"Go to the table; put the red book on top of the blue book."
"Go to the board; draw a line, erase it, bring the chalk to me."
"Pick up a book; open the book, give the open book to ____."
"Tell ____ to close the book."

Discrimination—Singular and Plural

Place several pictures of objects before the children, making sure that both the singular and plural of the critical word are illustrated. One series of pictures might include the following:

<u>bicycle</u>   buses   <u>bicycles</u>   clocks   shirt

Say, "I shall repeat one word several times, but I shall also say one word that is different. Listen for the different word and then find the picture that the different word is talking about."

train   train   bicycles   train   train

A child is called upon to find the picture that tells about the different word. He might say, "You said bicycles and here is a picture of some bicycles," or he might say, "Bicycles was the different word."

Further discussion can be directed toward the singular-plural concept. Bicycles mean more than one bicycle. Train means just one train. A skilled teacher can guide the more mature children into the enlarged concept of several cars and one engine being necessary to make <u>one train</u>, or <u>a train</u>.

Recalling Words Associated with a "Topic" or "Subject" Word

Refer to Promotion of Thought by Word Association on page 23, which should precede this exercise.

Name a familiar word to serve as the subject or thought, such as traffic, daddy, Christmas, pet, wagon, home.

Tell the children to <u>remember</u> the word and think of other words that this word makes them think about, such as:

traffic: cars, road, trucks, drivers
school: children, rooms, teacher, games, milk
buildings: house, school, garage, store

Frequently ask children to rename the topic word. Some children forget the word or get off the subject. They will need much practice.

Give clues to stimulate thought and word recall, such as:

"What do you play with at school?"

"What brings you to school?" (car, bus)

"What do you have in your room?"

In time, some children will be able to repeat the "topic" word and give several words that relate to it with no further help

Recognizing Irrelevant Sentences

Tell a simple little story. Include one irrelevant sentence. The children pick out the sentence that does not belong in the story.

Suggestions:

Tom has a new pet.
It is big and brown.
It wags its tail.
Mother likes to read.
Tom's pet is a dog.

A correct response by a child would be: "'Mother likes to read' does not belong in this story."

The mother bird began to build her nest.
The children played games at the party.
She used little sticks and twigs and leaves.
When the nest is finished the mother will lay her eggs.

It was Christmas Eve.
The children hung their stockings.
"Let us make some valentines," said Mary.
"Let us hurry into bed now," said Bobby.
"Santa will come when the children are asleep."

Children like to play.
They like to run and dance and sing.
Sometimes they play blocks.
Jane worked hard all day.
They like toy trains and dolls.

Mary's mother cat had some kittens.
This dog has a pretty collar.
The kittens jump all over the mother cat.
The mother cat plays with them.
Then she washes them with her tongue.

At the circus we see a big show.
This house is very large.
Clowns do funny tricks.
Animals are trained to do many entertaining stunts.
The band plays music during the show.

Betty ate the right food for breakfast.
She ate eggs and toast.
She always drank her milk.
Sometimes she had cereal and milk.
She ate only cake and ice cream.

PHONOLOGICAL AWARENESS

What is Phonological Awareness? In addition to developing a rich inner language, it is necessary for a child to develop the structure of language. Kindergarten children are usually eager to develop letter and number recognition. Direct instruction is required for the formation of letters, sound-symbol association, grouping of symbols with the corresponding sounds to form words, and grouping of words to express ideas.

Auditory analyses, often referred to as either phonological awareness or phonemic awareness, refers to the ability to recognize sounds in words and an awareness of the correct number of units, for example, the number of syllables within words.

Generally, phonological awareness is a more encompassing term than phonemic awareness. Torgesen (1993) provides the following definition: "Phonological awareness is one's sensitivity to, or explicit awareness of, the phonological structure of one's language It involves the ability to notice, think about, or manipulate, the individual sounds of words."

Hall and Moats (1999) describe phonemic awareness as being a narrower term than phonological awareness. Phonemic awareness refers to the ability to identify and manipulate individual sounds (phonemes) in words.

As discussed in the chapter on Language Development, most children begin to develop fairly sophisticated skills for auditory analysis early in life. They are able to recognize certain sound patterns well before their first birthdays. By three, they are able to discriminate and attach meaning to common words such as go, no, toe, nose, etc. It takes another three years before they are able to understand that spoken words not only have meaning, but also consist of separate components that are independent of semantics (Rosner 1993). It is believed that the recognition of phonemes requires the functional use of the kinesthetic movements of the child's own articulatory activities and is not merely an acoustical task developed by hearing the speech of others (Lindbloom 1989). Thus, the discovery of phonemes is usually a consequence of vocabulary growth. According to Premack (1972) "children cannot discover that sounds combine to have meanings until they discover that individual sounds have no meaning" (p. 65). Children become cognizant of words before phonemes, and they are usually able to isolate syllables before individual phonemes.

The ability to recognize and manipulate the position of these sound components (phonemes) within spoken words has been shown to be a key element in learning to read (Calfee, Lindamood, and Lindamood 1973; Stanovich 1986; Foorman, Francis, Shaywitz, Shaywitz, and Fletcher 1997; Foorman, Francis, Beeler, Winikates, and Fletcher 1997; Wagner, Torgesen, and Rashotte 1994). Likewise, the inability to identify and manipulate these sound components within words has been associated with difficulty in learning to read. For many, this phenomenon develops automatically and there is little awareness of its presence or importance. However, it is estimated that phonological awareness does not develop naturally in approximately 25% of the school-aged population. To rectify the problem, phonological awareness must be developed through direct instruction. Fortunately, experience has shown that these skills can be taught effectively by direct instruction using multisensory strategies such as the Slingerland Multisensory Approach to Language Arts or other Orton-Gillingham based multisensory programs (Slingerland 1996). Pre-reading activities to develop phonological awareness are contained within this chapter. It is suggested that children exhibiting the characteristics of specific lanuage disabilities (dyslexia) continue to receive instruction using the Slingerland Multisensory Approach to Language Arts[11] after completing these pre-reading activities.

Using Literature to Stimulate Phonological Awareness

Exposure to quality stories that rhyme and play with words is important in developing auditory skills, including phonological awareness. Children should be read to from the time of their birth. Reading in an animated voice and giving attention to proper phrasing provides children with the melody and rhythm of language. A number of the activities in this book involve literature. The following list should be considered just a beginning to the literature that you will want to provide to assist in developing children's listening (and later reading) skills.

Alda, A. 1992. *Sheep, Sheep, Sheep, Help Me Fall Asleep*. New York: Bantam Doubleday Dell Books for Young Readers.

Alda, A. 1994. *Pig, Horse, Cow, Don't Wake Me Now*. New York: Bantam Doubleday Dell Books for Young Readers.

Berenstain, S., and Berenstain, J. 1988. *The Berenstain Bears and the Ghost of the Forest*. New York: Random House, Inc.

Brown, M. 1994. *Pickle Things*. New York: Parents Magazine Press.

Brown, M.W. 1989. *Goodnight Moon*. New York: Scholastic Books.

Brown, M.W. 1993. *Four Fur Feet*. New York: Bantam Doubleday Dell Books for Young Readers.

Cole, J. 1989. *Anna Banana: 101 Jump Rope Rhymes*. New York: Morrow Junior Books.

Ehlert, L. 1989. *Eating the Alphabet: Fruits and Vegetables from A to Z*. San Diego: Harcourt Brace Jovanovich.

Ehlert, L. 1993. *Nuts to You*. San Diego: Harcourt Brace Jovanovich.

Martin, B. 1974. *Sounds of the Pow-Wow*. New York: Holt, Rinehart & Winston.

Martin, B., and Archambault, J. 1986. *Barn Dance*. New York: Holt, Rinehart & Winston.

Martin, B., and Archambault, J. 1987. *Here Are My Hands*. New York: Holt, Rinehart & Winston.

Martin, B., and Archambault, J. 1988. *Up and Down on the Merry-Go-Round*. New York: H. Holt & Co.

Martin, B., and Archambault, J. 1989. *Chicka Chicka Boom Boom*. New York: Simon & Schuster.

Martin, B., and Carle, E. 1991. *Polar Bear, Polar Bear, What Do you Hear?* New York: Simon & Schuster Books for Young Readers.

Patz, N. 1983. *Moses Supposes His Toeses are Roses*. San Diego: Harcourt Brace Jovanovich.

Sendak, M. 1990. *Alligators All Around: An Alphabet*. New York: Harper Trophy.

Seuss, Dr. 1960. *One Fish, Two Fish, Red Fish, Blue Fish*. New York: Beginner Books.

Seuss, Dr. 1965. *Fox in Socks*. New York: Random House.

Seuss, Dr. 1972. *In a People House*. New York: Random House.

Seuss, Dr. 1974. *There's a Wocket in My Pocket*. New York: Random House.

Seuss, Dr. 1991. *Dr. Seuss's ABC's* (2nd Ed.) New York: Random House.

Seuss, Dr. 1991. *My Many Colored Days*. New York: Alfred A Knopf, Inc. Random House.

Silverstein, S. 1964. *A Giraffe and a Half*. New York: Scholastic.

RHYMING

Rhyming is more difficult for some children than for others. Although rhyming is considered to be the easiest of the identified phonological tasks, it remains a challenge for many older children who suffer from dyslexia. They profit greatly from instruction in this important skill.

As children develop speech, they are concerned with "meaning" for communication, not with sounds. In rhyming the opposite is true; they must attend to the sounds of words, not the meaning. Exposure to rhyming experience and direct instruction at an early stage will assist in developing this skill. Hearing and re-hearing nursery rhymes assists the young child in this development. Unfortunately, in this day of TV-assisted childcare, frequent reading aloud and repetition of nursery rhymes is often neglected. Therefore, the first task is to provide opportunities for repeated exposure to these rhymes. This should be a daily activity. Your library or favorite bookstore has many selections to assist in this activity. Fortunately, young children enjoy rhymes and their repetition. They are quick to join rhyming activities when given the opportunity. As young as two years old, they have been observed to play a recorded phrase (in a toy) over and over until they can repeat it using the inflections of the speaker. Many of the rhymes can be sung and/or dramatized, as well as spoken.

Additional tasks to develop this skill include the following topics.

Rhyming—Nursery Rhymes—Listening for Rhyming Words

Using nursery rhymes, poems, and couplets, tell the children to listen for the rhyming words. It will be necessary to explain to them that the rhyming words will sound somewhat alike.

Children show "thumbs-up"[2] every time they hear the rhyming word. At first, it may be necessary to overemphasize the rhyming word. It is often necessary to repeat the rhyme several times before the children are able to distinguish the words that rhyme. You may even have to cue them by nodding your head or moving your hand or telling them the words that rhyme. Remember, the students are learning a new task, not being tested.

Children clap hands when they hear a rhyming word. Again, consider this a time of instruction using auditory emphasis and visual cues if necessary.

As a feeling for rhyming becomes established, the children may say the last one of the two rhyming words after you have said a couplet up to that word.

Examples: (Teacher says items in italics.)

Twinkle, twinkle little star
How I wonder what you _____. (Children say, "are.")

Later, an individual child may fill in both rhyming words as:

Twinkle, twinkle little ("star")
How I wonder what you ("are").

As a last step, you might say the entire rhyme and ask a child to name the two rhyming words, saying: "Star and are rhyme." "_____ and _____ rhyme."
Suggestions:

Hickory, dickory, dock
The mouse ran up the clock.

April showers
Bring May flowers.

The horse knows the way
To find the good hay.

These little girls
Have long golden curls.

Jack be nimble, Jack be quick,
Jack jump over the candlestick.

Captain, Captain, get your coat
And let's go sailing on your boat.

Busy, busy honeybee,
Buzzing in the honey tree.

Rhyming—Further Practice

The object of this exercise is to help children think of a rhyming word from context. The children are told to finish a couplet with a word that rhymes with the one at the end of the first line.
Suggested rhymes:

The sun is very bright.
It keeps us warm and gives us (light).

Bobby loves to jump and jump.
Down he comes with a great big (bump). (thump)

This little boy
Has a new (toy).

I think it is fun
To play and (run).

Some little girls
Wear their hair in (curls).

I saw a little mouse
Run into your doll (house).

In one sandwich I have jam.
In the other I have (ham).

Tommy caught this fine big fish.
Mother served it on a (dish).

The boys worked hard on the new shed
Till it was time to go to (bed).

Workers, workers here and there.
I see workers every (where).

Let's make the airfield in the sand
So all our planes come here to (land).

Mother is making a birthday cake.
She'll put it then in the oven to (bake).

It's fun to play in the park.
Hurry, quick, before it gets (dark).

Rhyme and Visual Association

FOLDER 18 Pictures of single objects
Naming Rhyming Pictures
Place three pictures or cards (from collection of real pictures or commercial reproductions such as Ideal Cards), two of which have rhyming names, on a table or a pocket chart. Ask a child to name all the pictures, then find the two pictures that have names that rhyme.

Matching Named Words with Rhyming Pictures
The children are told to listen to a word you say and then to look at the pictures to find one that rhymes with the word they have just heard.
Perhaps the pictures to be used are:

dog   house   toaster   girl   ball

Ask, "I'm looking for a picture whose name rhymes with <u>mouse</u>. Who can find it for me?"
When a child finds the right picture, he says the two rhyming words, "house, mouse."
Suggestions for pictures with rhyming words:

box	sox					
tree	bee					
sun	fun					
flower	tower	shower				
girls	whirls	curls	pearls			
kitten	mitten					
bed	bread	head	thread			
man	pan	tan	ran	fan		
boys	toys					
clock	rock	sock	top	shop	hop	mop
train	rain	cane				

Discriminating Rhyming Words

Pronounce three words, two of which rhyme. The children are to tell you the two rhyming words. Help the child to use a complete sentence: "Lamb and Sam rhyme." "___ and ___ rhyme."
Sample word list:

<u>dog</u>	<u>log</u>	cat
light	<u>book</u>	<u>look</u>
<u>bunny</u>	<u>funny</u>	butter
<u>sister</u>	<u>mister</u>	hard
<u>Dick</u>	<u>trick</u>	track
purple	<u>arm</u>	<u>farm</u>
food	<u>gum</u>	<u>drum</u>
sky	<u>tree</u>	<u>be</u>
<u>fly</u>	spoon	<u>tie</u>
man	<u>mother</u>	<u>brother</u>
ouch	<u>house</u>	<u>mouse</u>
just	<u>duck</u>	<u>truck</u>
<u>girl</u>	hurt	<u>curl</u>
<u>top</u>	tall	<u>hop</u>
<u>same</u>	<u>came</u>	take

foot	<u>feet</u>	<u>meet</u>
<u>lady</u>	sister	<u>shady</u>
<u>keep</u>	last	<u>sleep</u>
<u>toy</u>	head	<u>boy</u>
<u>beach</u>	eat	<u>peach</u>
<u>lamb</u>	<u>Sam</u>	bed

More Rhyming Practice

"Today we are going to make up some rhymes. You will need to help think of words to rhyme with my word."

Samples:

(Emphasize rhyming word.)

"I saw a <u>cat</u> chase a _____." (rat, bat, hat, etc.)

"The <u>snake</u> hid behind the _____." (rake, cake, etc.)

"My <u>teddy</u> is named _____." (Heddy, Freddie, etc.)

"What can we <u>make</u>? A great big _____." (cake, lake, etc.)

"See the <u>lark</u> singing in the _____." (park, dark)

"The little <u>mouse</u> lives in a great big _____." (house)

"Let's <u>go</u> play in the ____." (snow)

"If you want the boat to <u>go, go, go,</u> you have to _____." (row, row, row)

"She's in the <u>mood</u> to eat a lot of _____." (food)

"Put the <u>nail</u> in the shiny _____." (pail)

Rhyming Game—"Spin the Bottle"

Children should sit in a circle on the floor. The game begins with you saying a simple, one-syllable word and spinning the bottle. When the bottle stops, the child in front of the open end of the bottle gives a rhyming word. If the child is successful in giving a rhyming word, he or she will give the next spin after you have given the next word to be rhymed. If the child cannot think of a rhyming word the bottle is spun again by the previous "spinner" and someone else will have a turn. After the children become adept at this, they may be able to supply the stimulus word.

Rhyming Games—"Roll the Ball" or "Toss the Bean Bag"

These games are played in the same manner as "Spin the Bottle" except rolling a ball or tossing a bean bag is used to select the next participant. Children should sit in a circle on the floor. The game begins with you saying a simple, one-syllable word and rolling the ball or tossing the bean bag to a child. The receiving child gives a rhyming word. Then the child sends the ball or bean bag back to you. After the children become adept at this, they may be able to supply the stimulus word and direct the ball or bean bag to another child. At first, however, it should go to you. This allows you to ensure success for the participants by carefully matching the rhyming word with the child's ability level.

Rhyming—Roll Call or Dismissal to Activity Centers

After the children are comfortable with rhyming, give each child a rhyming word when calling roll or dismissing to a center, etc. The child responds with a rhyming word.

Example:
Teacher: "Mary, your word is 'hop.'"
Mary: "'Top' rhymes with 'hop.'"

Composing Group Rhymes

In this activity, you work with the class to develop a language experience poem, which rhymes.

"Today we are going to make up a rhyme telling what we like to do on a sunny day. I will help you get started. Then we will all work together to make up the rhyme. Listen carefully."

Write these words on large chart paper: "On a bright, sunny day." Gently lead the students as they develop a simple rhyme. This can be accomplished by asking questions such as: "Whom will our rhyme be about?"

Other guiding questions can pertain to when, where, how, or what. Give children an opportunity to respond. Perhaps the rhyme will proceed as follows:

"That is a good suggestion. We will make this rhyme about all the children."

"On a bright, sunny day, all the children . . ."

Continue recording the rhyme on the chart.

"What do they do? Remember that it needs to rhyme with 'day.' Can you think of a word that rhymes with day?" Underline the word day.

Perhaps the group will end up with something like, "On a bright, sunny day, all the children go out to play."

When the composition is completed, various children are given the opportunity to repeat the rhyme. (This also strengthens auditory memory). Record the rhyme and post it in the room or place it in a "group rhyme book."

Keep adding to your list of rhyme starters. Some suggestions to begin with are:

There was a little fish . . .
On a cold, dark night . . .
We went to the park . . .
I had a little hen . . .

Composing Group Rhymes is also a good exercise for older students. It is especially helpful for older children with specific language disabilities (dyslexia), as many of them have not developed a "sense" of rhyming. Have fun with this activity as some fourth grade students at The Prentice School, a non-profit school for dyslexic students, did with the following poem.

I Made a Mistake

I went to the bathroom to wash my hands.
I made a mistake and washed the pans.

I went to the pet shop to pick up a dog
I made a mistake and kissed a frog.

I went to the store to buy a toy
I made a mistake and bought a koi.

I went to the park to build an ark
I made a mistake and built Mr. Clark.

1/27/2000 Mrs. Burtrum's Class
First published in *The Prentice Post*
The Prentice School, Santa Ana, California

Discrimination of Same and Different Words

Ask the children to listen while you say some words. Tell them that one word will sound different or not the same, and that they are to listen carefully so they can discover which word is different. At first, the "different" word should be readily apparent as in the examples below:

man	man	man	<u>boy</u>	man
play	<u>fun</u>	play	play	play
house	house	<u>horse</u>	house	house
snow	snow	snow	snow	<u>sky</u>
bush	bush	<u>tree</u>	bush	bush
water	water	water	<u>river</u>	water

Discrimination—Similar Words with Changing Phonemes

The need for listening is increased by changing the initial consonant sounds, or the final consonant sounds, or by changing the vowel sounds.

run	run	<u>sun</u>	run	run
<u>rub</u>	tub	tub	tub	tub
chick	chick	chick	<u>stick</u>	chick
truck	truck	truck	truck	<u>cluck</u>
skip	skip	<u>skim</u>	skip	skip
pat	pat	pat	pat	<u>pan</u>
each	each	each	<u>east</u>	each
<u>hush</u>	hunt	hunt	hunt	hunt
hid	hid	hid	<u>had</u>	hid
coat	coat	<u>kite</u>	coat	coat
jump	<u>bump</u>	jump	jump	jump
wish	wish	wish	<u>fish</u>	wish
stand	stand	<u>grand</u>	stand	stand
flower	<u>shower</u>	flower	flower	flower
run	run	<u>rug</u>	run	run
load	<u>loaf</u>	load	load	load
limp	limp	<u>list</u>	limp	limp
west	west	west	<u>went</u>	west
drank	drank	drank	<u>drink</u>	drank
left	<u>lift</u>	left	left	left

Discrimination of Words with Action Response

As a variation of Discrimination—Similar Words with Changing Phonemes on this page, tell the children to "Listen for the word that is different, and to do what it says."

rip	rip	rip	<u>skip</u>	rip
fun	<u>run</u>	fun	fun	fun
loop	loop	<u>stoop</u>	loop	loop
peach	<u>reach</u>	peach	peach	peach
shop	shop	<u>hop</u>	shop	shop
bump	bump	bump	<u>jump</u>	bump

talk	talk	<u>walk</u>	talk	talk
round	round	round	<u>pound</u>	round

Use short sentences sometimes instead of single words:

Run to the window.	Run to the window.	<u>Run to the door.</u>	Run to the window.
Touch your knee.	Touch your knee.	Touch your knee.	<u>Touch your head.</u>
<u>Cover your eyes.</u>	Shut your eyes.	Shut your eyes.	Shut your eyes.
Skip to the door.	Skip to the door.	<u>Skip to the easel.</u>	Skip to the door.
Wave your hand.	Wave your hand.	<u>Wave your hands.</u>	Wave your hand.
Walk around the room.	Walk around the room.	Walk around the room.	<u>Walk around the table.</u>

Word Discrimination—Auditory-Visual Association

FOLDER 18

Take the pictures from the Folder and place four or five of them before the children, saying, "I am going to say some words. All but one will sound alike. Listen for the one that sounds different and then find the picture that word is about."

<u>Do not assume that children understand the meaning of "alike" and "different."</u> This concept should be checked to determine whether children are ready to do this exercise without further clarification. Be sure that the "different" word is represented by one of the pictures exposed to the children.

The child designated to find the picture responds in a complete sentence such as, "The different word was bicycle," or "Bicycle is not like the other words."

When a child cannot answer in a sentence but says, "Bicycle," casually tell him that the way to tell his classmates would be to say: "The different word was bicycle." Have the child repeat. Let the group repeat the word, thus patterning speech for all children.

You should constantly be adding to your collection of pictures.

Suggestions:

stove	stove	stove	<u>sink</u>
horse	horse	<u>house</u>	horse
roast	<u>toast</u>	roast	roast
bicycle	bicycle	<u>ship</u>	bicycle

Same and Different Sound Discrimination—Individual Phonemes

Teacher: "Today, I want you to listen as I make some different sounds. See if you and I made the same sound each time, or if I made different sounds. If I make the same sound each time, give me a "thumbs up." Demonstrate forming a fist with thumb sticking up.

"If the sounds are different, give a thumbs down." Demonstrate thumbs down. "Now, let's practice. Show me the sign for sounds that are the same. Show me the sign for sounds that are different. Listen carefully . . . sounds that are the same . . . sounds that are different." Practice until you are sure the children understand the signs.

"We are ready to begin. I will say three sounds. Show me with your thumbs up if all three sounds are the same or thumbs down if they are different."

As you begin these exercises, let children watch your face for visual cues. On later days, cover your mouth so that discrimination is limited to hearing differences. You will then become aware of the students who need the visual cues. This is good as a filler or transition activity.

Several short sessions with high attention are better than having one long session.

/m/	/m/	/m/	/s/	/s/	/s/
/l/	/l/	/m/	/k/	/s/	/k/
/t/	/t/	/d/	/t/	/t/	/t/
/b/	/b/	/d/	/n/	/n/	/n/
/s/	/s/	/z/	/s/	/z/	/s/
/k/	/k/	/sh/	/f/	/f/	/f/
/f/	/f/	/v/	/ch/	/p/	/p/
/r/	/r/	/r/	/r/	/r/	/wh/
/d/	/d/	/p/	/sh/	/sh/	/ck/

Recognition of Same Sounds (Phonemes) at Beginning of Words

"Today we are going to play a game with our ears. Listen carefully and see if you can tell me which words begin with the same sound." At this time, no attempt is made to name the letter.

Be careful to enunciate the sounds clearly and correctly.

If a child volunteers the letter name, say, "Yes, that sound is made by the letter__" and write the letter on the board. "Soon we will be learning all about many letters. Today, let's just listen for the words that have the same sound." (It is important to keep your focus on the objective of the lesson.)

<u>big</u>   <u>bun</u>   man

"Which two words begin with the same sound?" Child responds.

Teacher: "Yes, big and bun begin with the sound /b/." (Continue reinforcing sound.) "Can you tell me about the two words in a sentence?"

Child: "The words big and bun begin with the same sound."

dog   <u>cot</u>   <u>can</u>

Child: "The words <u>cot</u> and <u>can</u> begin with the same sound."
Teacher: "Yes, <u>cot</u> and <u>can</u> begin with the sound /k/."
(Continue dialogue as stated above.)

<u>run</u>	sun	<u>ride</u>
<u>call</u>	fan	<u>cat</u>
<u>dig</u>	<u>dog</u>	big
<u>fix</u>	<u>fig</u>	vest
<u>man</u>	sand	<u>mug</u>
<u>check</u>	stall	<u>chop</u>
<u>wish</u>	dash	<u>wig</u>
win	<u>net</u>	<u>no</u>
<u>lamp</u>	thin	<u>lug</u>
<u>rig</u>	beg	<u>rust</u>
<u>vim</u>	<u>vigor</u>	Ben
<u>sag</u>	fist	<u>sip</u>
<u>lap</u>	snap	<u>light</u>
raft	<u>list</u>	<u>left</u>
<u>west</u>	rent	<u>wept</u>

More Recognition of Same Sounds at Beginning of Words

"Again, today we are going to play the game with our ears. Listen carefully and see if you can tell me which words begin with the same sound." At this time, no attempt is made to name the letter. If a child volunteers the letter name, you should say, "Yes, that sound is made by the letter___" and write the letter on the board. "Soon we will be learning all about many letters. Today, let's just listen for the words that have the same sound." (It is important to keep your focus on the objective of the lesson. It is tempting to jump ahead before the children have truly developed the skill.)

> quit   <u>wit</u>   <u>wish</u>

Teacher: "Which two words begin with the same sound?"
Child: "The words <u>wit</u> and <u>wish</u> begin with the same sound."
Teacher: "Yes, <u>wit</u> and <u>wish</u> begin with the sound /w/."
> (Continue dialogue as stated above.)

<u>mum</u>	pun	<u>mop</u>
<u>dug</u>	hug	<u>dust</u>
<u>rum</u>	<u>rug</u>	tut
<u>hut</u>	<u>hunt</u>	cut
crib	<u>mix</u>	<u>mitt</u>
<u>pick</u>	<u>pig</u>	nix
<u>goat</u>	boat	<u>gun</u>
<u>chug</u>	cult	<u>chum</u>
<u>wax</u>	gas	<u>wick</u>
<u>camp</u>	sash	<u>clang</u>
<u>fast</u>	<u>flat</u>	pass
<u>hasp</u>	<u>ham</u>	tan
<u>mash</u>	nash	<u>map</u>
mad	<u>nap</u>	<u>name</u>
<u>add</u>	<u>ash</u>	dash
gas	<u>jab</u>	<u>jacks</u>

Recognition of Sounds (Phonemes) at the Beginning of Names

Explain to the children that today they are going to play a guessing game with the sounds they hear at the beginning of their names. When they think that they know the name, they are to give the "thumbs-up" signal. If they think that it is the beginning sound in their name they should raise their hands. The beginning sound should be given clearly. If the child does not recognize the sound (and some will not), you may cue the one child by looking directly at him or her and making the sound. If the child still doesn't recognize the sound, say, "/t/ as in Tommy," exaggerating the sound /t/ in the word Tommy. This game should be repeated on a number of different days.

Beginning Sounds of Names Used to Dismiss Children

A variation of the previous game is to dismiss children to activity centers, recess, etc. by giving the sound at the beginning of their names.
> Example:
> Teacher: "If your name begins with this sound, /t/, you may quietly get your milk and go to (name activity center)."

If after repeating the sound several times a child does not recognize it as beginning his name, go on to another sound and come back to him a little later.

Recognition of Same Phonemes at the End of Words

"Today, we are going to play our listening game in a different way. Listen carefully and see if you can tell me which words end with the same sound. Listen for the very last sound you hear. If I say the word <u>cat</u>, it begins with the sound /k/. What sound do you hear at the very end of the word <u>cat</u>?" /t/

It is helpful for you to use your hand in a left to right motion, demonstrating the beginning and end of a word. The hand is then used to emphasize the last sound. Again, no attempt is made to name the letter at this time. It is much easier for a child to identify the beginning sound than it is to isolate and identify the final sound in words. Research (Lieberman 1985) has indicated that the ratio of errors of final sounds to initial or beginning sounds is 2:1. You will probably need to do this exercise on several days. Keep practice sessions short and carefully paced.

<u>pod</u>   <u>rod</u>   trot

Teacher: "Which two words end with the same sound?"
Child: "The words <u>pod</u> and <u>rod</u> end with the same sound."
Teacher: "Yes, <u>pod</u> and <u>rod</u> both end with the sound /d/."
(Continue dialogue as stated above.)

<u>spot</u>	<u>mutt</u>	dog
<u>hot</u>	hod	<u>slot</u>
<u>man</u>	<u>fan</u>	dad
<u>tot</u>	tall	<u>lot</u>
<u>lisp</u>	spit	<u>lip</u>
<u>crib</u>	creek	<u>crab</u>
<u>flit</u>	<u>flat</u>	flash
<u>tuft</u>	<u>taft</u>	tug
<u>fond</u>	fun	<u>fund</u>
<u>much</u>	<u>bench</u>	chin
<u>staff</u>	stub	<u>stiff</u>
ramp	<u>brand</u>	<u>land</u>

More Recognition of Same Phonemes at the End of Words

Teacher: "Today, we are going to play our listening game again. Listen carefully and see if you can tell me which words end with the same sound. Listen for the very last sound you hear. If I say the word <u>dog</u>, it begins with the sound /d/. What sound do you hear at the very end of the word <u>dog</u>?"

Teacher: "<u>Stock</u>, <u>flop</u>, <u>stack</u>. Which two words end with the same sound?"
Child: "The words <u>stock</u> and <u>stack</u> end with the same sound."
Teacher: "Yes, both <u>stock</u> and <u>stack</u> end with the sound /k/."
(Continue dialogue as stated above.)

<u>spot</u>	<u>mutt</u>	dog
<u>romp</u>	run	<u>stump</u>
<u>sprint</u>	sprig	<u>spent</u>

fat	mag	mat
wig	wag	pig
gag	gap	gig
fib	fan	pan
spin	sped	sled
gnat	net	Ned
dab	bib	dash
check	chin	chick
grip	whip	tam
quest	quit	quim
raft	rift	rag
chap	chaff	crisp
wish	dash	sham
dish	torch	wish

Discrimination of Specified Initial Phonemes

The purpose of this exercise is to continue to develop auditory discrimination. This is a preparatory step, which will assist in the later recognition of specific sounds and their association with letters (graphemes). The children will not be expected to learn the letter names at this time. In the near future, a letter will be named and the formation of the letter, along with its name and the sound, will be carefully taught.

Teacher: "Today, I am going to name some words. If you hear the /h/ sound at the beginning of the word, give me a "thumbs up." (Refer to "thumbs up" procedure taught during rhyming.)

/h/

hat	hair	ball	haul	honey
tall	hurry	hug	keep	heap
high	bye	hen	hot	hum

/s/

say	sand	can	see	side
ride	same	soap	cat	sat
Sam	ham	sick	swing	slide

/m/

me	much	money	bunny	man
pan	mice	moon	nuts	make
mud	mold	old	men	must

/r/

rug	rag	rock	knock	rub
tub	rat	rich	rake	take
rim	rust	bust	rig	roast

/t/

to	toy	boy	tag	take
tooth	top	hop	time	tug
bunny	tummy	tick	talk	tan

/b/

bear	bath	ball	tall	big
bed	boat	coat	buzz	bell
bust	bank	boy	bother	break

/g/ (hard sound)

goat	boat	go	game	girl
garden	good	hood	gas	goose
gate	get	gum	bold	gold

Guessing Game—Words to Contain a Specified Sound

(These activities are to be used over a number of days.)

Choose a particular sound, such as long vowel sound /oo/, and say, "We are going to play a game with our ears and heads. I am going to ask you some questions and you are to answer with a word containing the sound /oo/. What do you know that shines in the sky?"

Perhaps <u>moon</u> will be thought of immediately but maybe some child will say star. If that happens, say, "It is true a star is in the sky, but the word you want must have the sound /oo/ in it. A star is not called a stoo. What else can you think of that shines in the sky and has the sound /oo/?"

Other suggestions for the sound /oo/:

"With what do we eat ice cream?" (spoon)

"What do we call the things Daddy uses when he builds a playhouse?" (tools)

"To grow and be strong what must all children eat?" (food)

"What do we say chickens do when they go to bed?" (roost)

"I am thinking of something children like to swim in and it is not the ocean. What is it?" (pool)

"Sometimes children wear mittens on their hands. What do they wear on their feet?" (shoes, boots) (oe says /oo/ in the word shoes)

"When boys and girls are growing up, something has to be pulled out of their mouths sometimes. What is it?" (tooth)

"Before your tooth gets pulled out, how does it usually feel when you touch it?" (loose)

Suggestions for other sounds to be used in questions on other days:

/ar/

c<u>ar</u>	t<u>ar</u>	p<u>ar</u>ty	b<u>ar</u>k	p<u>ar</u>k
sh<u>ar</u>k	sp<u>ar</u>k	b<u>ar</u>n	f<u>ar</u>m	d<u>ar</u>k

/oi/

b<u>oy</u>	j<u>oy</u>	<u>oi</u>l	b<u>oi</u>l	c<u>oi</u>n
t<u>oy</u>	n<u>oi</u>se	h<u>oi</u>st	s<u>oi</u>l	

/ou/

<u>ou</u>t	sh<u>ou</u>t	r<u>ou</u>nd	p<u>ou</u>nd	p<u>ou</u>t
cr<u>ow</u>d	cl<u>ow</u>n	m<u>ou</u>se	d<u>ow</u>n	

/a/

t<u>ai</u>l	r<u>a</u>ke	n<u>a</u>me	p<u>a</u>ste	n<u>ai</u>l
sh<u>a</u>de	ch<u>ai</u>r	pl<u>ay</u>	tr<u>ai</u>l	c<u>a</u>ke

/e/

sheep	peach	weeds	cream	meat
steam	seeds	feet	beets	

/i/

mice	pie	night	sky	knife	spine
light	bright	fly	white		

/o/

coat	boat	home	roast	coast
post	pole	toast	toes	

/u/

mule	cute	use	fuel	fuse

/a/

pad	fan	cap	lad	catch	match
Dad	lamb	stamp	wag	gas	

/e/

bed	tent	step	den	sled	shed
dress	head	red	chest		

/i/

pin	fist	wrist	wish	ship
chin	lid	trip	Jim	rib

/o/

top	lock	fox	Don	shock	clock
pond	rocks	mop	box		

/u/

hunt	chum	rust	dust	cuff
muff	crust	fun	tub	cut

/sh/

ship	shore	shells	show	wish
dish	shade	shop	fish	

/wh/

whale	wheel	whip	whistle	wheat	white

/ch/

chair	chin	cheese	cheek	chain	chicken

/th/

thorn	thank	thin	thick	think

Synthesizing Compound Words

Synthesizing or "blending" of sounds into words will begin with compound words, as this will be easier than smaller, less meaningful units. Children are physically able to discriminate between words before they can discriminate between syllables, and syllables before individual phonemes (sounds) (Lieberman 1974). Children should repeat words aloud. It is thought that it is not just hearing the sounds, but also the kinesthetic motor movements needed to reproduce these sounds, that is important in helping children develop phonological awareness (Calvin and Ojemann 1980).

Explain to the children that you are going to say some words that they know. However, you are going to say them in parts, and the children are to try and guess the whole secret word. Then pronounce a familiar compound word, pausing briefly between each part or syllable. As you do so, move your arm in arch fashion to demonstrate each part of the word.

Example:

Teacher:

"Sand" (hand makes arch) Pause.

"Box" (hand makes another arch)

Teacher: "Now, say the words after me. Sand."

Children: "Sand."

Teacher: "Box."

Children: "Box."

Teacher: "Now, put the two words together, starting with the word sand."

Children: "Sandbox."

Use your voice to help the children blend words together during this learning example.

Teacher: "When we put these two words together they say sandbox (using hand to put the two parts together into one arch). Let's try some more words."

Sample Words:

toy	box	toybox	play	ground	playground
camp	ground	campground	mail	man	mailman
fire	man	fireman	farm	house	farmhouse
band	stand	bandstand	out	side	outside
in	to	into	in	side	inside
box	top	boxtop	cat	nip	catnip
flint	stone	flintstone	up	on	upon

Synthesizing Familiar Words—Names

As you proceed to synthesizing smaller units, it is helpful to begin by using very familiar words, such as the names of the children in the class.

Explain that they are going to play the Secret Word Guessing Game again. This time, they will try to guess whose name you are saying. It is suggested that you use the names of the students in the class for this exercise. Again, you may wish to move your arm in arches as you name syllables. Begin with words of more than one syllable.

Sample names:

Car	los		Carlos	Da	vid		David
Penn	y		Penny	Li	sa		Lisa
Mar	y		Mary	Deb	ra		Debra
Kar	en		Karen	Car	o	lyn	Carolyn
Kim	ber	ly	Kimberly	Ma	ri	a	Maria
Jo	se		Jose	Es	tel	la	Estella
Fer	nan	do	Fernando	Brit	tan	y	Brittany
Stan	ley		Stanley	Bar	bra		Barbra

Will	iam	William		Br		ett	Brett
Sue		Sue		Fr	ank		Frank
Fr	ed	Fred		Tra	cy		Tracy
Car	ol	Carol		M	ar	k	Mark
B	ob	Bob		K	i	m	Kim
J	on	Jon/John		T	e	d	Ted
Vic	tor	Victor					

Synthesizing Familiar Words—Auditory/Visual Association

This game is a continuation of the exercises in the two previous activities. Explain that they are going to play another word game today: "We are going to add a sound to a word to make a new word. Try to guess the word." Clearly give sounds and assist students in blending the sounds into a word.

Don't expect students to read the word. The goal of this game is to assist the students in synthesizing sounds and recognizing the sound-symbol relationships in preparation for future reading.

You should write the word on the board. As you make new sounds, you write the sound's corresponding graphemes (letter) to the left of the word. As the children synthesize or blend the sounds together, draw an arch under the new grapheme (letter) representation of the initial sound and the letters of the original word. After a word is synthesized, write the new word.

Sample Words:

	it			at	
b	it	bit	b	at	bat
s	it	sit	s	at	sat
h	it	hit	h	at	hat
f	it	fit	f	at	fat
l	it	lit	p	at	pat
w	it	wit	m	at	mat
qu	it	quit	t	at	tat
p	it	pit	c	at	cat
k	it	kit	r	at	rat

	in			old	
ch	in	chin	b	old	bold
t	in	tin	t	old	told
b	in	bin	f	old	fold
f	in	fin	s	old	sold
sh	in	shin	m	old	mold
th	in	thin	c	old	cold
w	in	win	g	old	gold
k	in	kin	h	old	hold
s	in	sin			

Synthesizing More Familiar Words

This game is a continuation of the exercises in the previous games. Explain that they are going to play another word game today and that the children should try to guess your secret word. Clearly give sounds and assist students in blending the sounds into a word. If the children have difficulty, it is helpful for you to extend or lengthen the sounds and blend through the vowel, then allow the students to finish the word.

While using your hand in an arching movement to reinforce the idea of blending sounds together and not letting the sounds stop, be sure that the hand forms an arch that only extends over syllables, not individual sounds.

Sample words:

/b	all/		ball
/t	all/		tall
/f	all/		fall
/t	oy/		toy
/b	oy/		boy
/d	o	ll/	doll
/k	a	t/	cat
/s	a	t/	sat
/l	a	g/	lag
/l	a	b/	lab
/t	a	g/	tag
/d	a	d/	dad
/m	a	d/	mad
/s	a	d/	sad
/h	i	m/	him
/h	i	t/	hit
/p	i	t/	pit
/p	i	n/	pin
/p	i	g/	pig

No attempt is made to attach the letter names to the sounds at this time.

More Practice in Synthesizing Familiar Words

This game is a continuation of the sound synthesizing exercises. Explain that they are going to play another word game today and that the children should try to guess your secret word. Clearly give sounds and assist students in blending the sounds into a word. If the children have difficulty, it is helpful for you to extend or lengthen the sounds and blend through the vowel, then allow the students to finish the word.

Sample Words:

/m	o	m/		mom
/r	u	n/		run
/j	u	m	p/	jump
/b	ea	ch/		beach
/p	ar	k/		park
/r	a	ce/		race
/k	a	ke/		cake
/t	o	p/		top
/s	t	o	p/	stop
/p	l	ay/		play
/d	r	e	ss/	dress
/s	w	i	m/	swim
/k	a	m	p/	camp

This game should be repeated a number of times on different days using different words. No attempt is made to attach the sounds to letters <u>at this time</u>.

Recognition of Sound Units—Number of Words in Phrases

The teachers explains, "Today, I am going to say a group of words. When I finish, it will be your turn to repeat what I said."

Teacher: "A red car."

Children: "A red car."

Teacher: "Good, now say it again and see if you can tell me how many words we said. Listen closely and count the words. Are you ready? Let's count them by holding up one finger for each word."

Lead group in saying the words "a red car" as the children raise fingers.

"How many words did we say?"

As you finish, each child should be holding up three fingers. If some are still having difficulty, work a few more phrases out together. If the children understand the exercise, they are ready to become more independent.

Teacher: "This time, I don't want you to say the answer, but show me by holding up the correct number of fingers to show how many words I said."

Say a phrase. Children repeat and hold up correct number of fingers to indicate words in phrases.

Sample Phrases:

<u>who</u>	the big boy	3
	the old man	3
	Bob and Bill	3
	three girls	2
	the teacher	2
<u>where</u>	in the forest	3
	down the road	3
	at the brown house	4
	at the circus	3
	on the big table	4
	in the white box	4
	by the chair	3
<u>when</u>	last night	2
	early this morning	3
	at noon	2
	during recess	2
	once upon a time	4
<u>action</u>	ran and ran	3
	jumped high	2
	saw the movie	3
	talked and talked	3
	smiled	1
	is smiling	2
	can smile	2
	smiles	1

Recognition of Sound Units—Number of Words in Sentences

Explain, "Today, I am going to say some sentences and we are going to see if you can tell me how many words I said. Remember to hold up your fingers as you count the words. I will know that you have the correct number by seeing how many fingers you are holding up. Are you ready? Listen closely and count the words in these sentences."

Sample Sentences:

The boy jumps.	3
Run after the ball.	4
We are friends.	3
The big cat purred.	4
He ran quickly.	3
The car can stop and go.	6
She skipped up the stairs.	5
Fernando went to the park.	5
He jumped down.	3
Run, Tom, run.	3
Anna is good at reading.	5
Mary walked home.	3
David hit the ball.	4
The boys went in the house.	6
The cat chased the mouse.	5
Sally and Beth are friends.	5
Miguel likes to play ball.	5

Recognition of Sound Units—Number of Syllables in Words

Prior to beginning this task, be sure that the students have had ample practice in recognizing words in phrases and sentences. This should be a small group activity that is continued for several days.

Teacher: "Today, we are going to play a new game. Let's have everyone put your hands under your chins." (Demonstrate placing hand, palm side down, just below chin.)

"Now repeat the word pardon."

Children repeat pardon.

Teacher: "How many times did your chins come down and touch your hand when you said pardon?"

Children respond.

Teacher: "That's right—two times." Draw a straight line on the board as you say each syllable of pardon." (Note: The children will be using straight lines to represent each syllable in later blending and spelling exercises when being taught with the Slingerland Multisensory Approach to Language Arts.)

Teacher: "What did this first line (pointing to first straight line) say?"

Children: "par."

Teacher: "What did this next line say?"

Children: "don."

Teacher: "When we put them together, what did they say?"

Children respond with "pardon."

Teacher: "Now, let's try some other words."

Children may respond in several different ways other than just raising their hands and telling the answer. If they are working with colored lima beans, cubes, or other markers, they may put the correct number of markers in front of them.

They may also put up the correct number of fingers.

Reinforce visually by drawing a dash on the board as you say each syllable. Children then recall each syllable as you point to each straight line. Then, syllables are put together as they were in the example.

cat/nip	2		ta/ble	2
ten/nis	2		post/man	2
riv/er	2		moun/tain	2
road	1		free/way	2
jel/lo	2		pud/ding	2
cake	1		fruit	1
play	1		tel/e/phone	3
fan/tas/tic	3		play/ful	2
tram/po/line	3		swing	1
in/vi/ta/tion	4		par/ty	2
Jan/u/ar/y	4		Feb/ru/ar/y	4
March	1		A/pril	2
June	1		Ju/ly	2
Au/gust	2		Sep/tem/ber	3
Oc/to/ber	3		No/vem/ber	3
De/cem/ber	3		Mon/day	2
Tues/day	2		Thurs/day	2
Fri/day	2		Sat/ur/day	3
Sun/day	2		hol/i/day	3
to/day	2		(Wednesday omitted due to difficulty in hearing syllables)	
Chris/tmas	2		hal/lo/ween	3
val/en/tine	3		Eas/ter	2
Han/u/kah	3		school	1
pre/pare	2		tur/key	2
ham/bur/ger	3		po/ta/toes	3
corn	1		fruit	1
on/ly	2		chil/dren	2
teach/er	2		prin/ci/pal	3
in/vent	2		fun	1
to/mor/row	3		yes/ter/day	3
choose	1		tel/e/phone	3
num/ber	2		a/ddress	2
el/e/phant	3		bears	1
flow/er	2		rose	1
ap/ple	2		ba/nan/a	3
mar/ket	2		store	1
in/for/ma/tion	4		chair	1
con/tain/ing	3		in/ven/tion	3

re/cess	2	con/fer/ence	3
tel/e/vi/sion	4	ham/mer	2
spi/der	2	mon/key	2

Recognizing Sound Units—Number of Syllables in Students' Names.

Teacher: "Today, we are going to count the syllables or word parts in our names. My name is _____."

Let's see if we can figure out how many syllables are in my name.

Do you remember how we count the syllables? Please put your hands under your chins." (Demonstrate placing hands, palm side down just below the chin.)

"Now repeat my name, _____."

Children repeat, "_____."

Teacher: "How many times did your chins come down and touch your hands when you said _____?"

Children respond.

Teacher: "That's right, ___ times."

Draw a straight line on the board as you say each syllable of your name ___. "What did this first line (pointing to first straight line) say?"

Children respond.

"What did the next line say? When we put them together, what name do they say? Now let's try some other names. When it's your turn, you should say: <u>My name is Bobby. Please say my name with me. Bobby. My name has two syllables: Bob by. Bobby.</u>"

Give children the opportunity to work out their own names.

If working in a large group, it may be necessary to do this activity over several days. Watch pacing and interest level. It is better to have short, high-quality working periods than to try to cover too much. This could cause children to lose interest or become frustrated or discouraged

Omitting Units of Sounds—Letters in Folksong "BINGO"

The children's song BINGO will be used to help children learn to omit or leave out sound units.

The first verse is sung as follows:

There was a farmer, had a dog,
And Bingo was his name-oh.
B-I-N-G-O, B-I-N-G-O, B-I-N-G-O,
And Bingo was his name-oh.

During the next verses, the singing of the letter name marked with an X will be omitted and singers will clap in its place. Instruct children to "think the letter names in their heads" when they clap.

There was a farmer, had a dog,
And Bingo was his name-oh.
B-I-N-G-X, B-I-N-G-X, B-I-N-G-X,
And Bingo was his name-oh.

There was a farmer, had a dog,
And Bingo was his name-oh.
B-I-N-X-X, B-I-N-X-X, B-I-N-X-X,
And Bingo was his name-oh.

There was a farmer, had a dog,
And Bingo was his name-oh.
B-I-X-X-X, B-I-X-X-X, B-I-X-X-X,
And Bingo was his name-oh.

There was a farmer, had a dog,
And Bingo was his name-oh.
B-X-X-X-X, B-X-X-X-X, B-X-X-X-X
And Bingo was his name-oh.

There was a farmer, had a dog,
And Bingo was his name-oh.
X-X-X-X-X, X-X-X-X-X, X-X-X-X-X
And Bingo was his name-oh.

Recognizing Embedded Words in Compound Words

This activity will be introduced by using the larger units, compound words. The objective is for children to be able to hold a stimulus word in memory and recognize its sequence of sound units.

Review the song BINGO in preparation for activities to follow in the next few days.

Teacher: "This game is called the Hidden Word Game. I will say a long word. There may be a little word hidden in the long word."

Teacher: "Say the word catnip. Did you hear the hidden word cat in the word catnip? Now say the word catnip again. Did you hear the word nip hidden in the word catnip?" Continue working with compound words in the following list.

Teacher's Script:
1. "Say the word catnip."
2. "Did you hear the word cat in the word catnip?"
3. "Was the word cat in the beginning or at the end of the word?"

1.	2.	3.
catnip	cat	beginning
catnip	nip	end
mailbox	mail	beginning
mailbox	box	end
doghouse	house	end
doghouse	dog	beginning
into	to	end
into	in	beginning
outside	side	end
outside	out	beginning
airplane	air	beginning
airplane	plane	end

Recognizing Missing Units of Sound from Compound Words

Again, this activity will be introduced by using the larger unit, compound words. The objective is for the children to be able to hold the stimulus word in memory and recognize the sequence of sound units within a familiar, compound word, omit a given sound unit, and pronounce the remaining sound unit or units. As this skill is developed, the task will gradually move through smaller units to the individual phonemes. These are more difficult for the children to discriminate within the larger word unit. It should be understood that this task will be difficult for some children, especially those who may have a language disability. You should maintain a relaxed, positive manner while working with the students and move at their pace. Be sure the children understand the task at the compound word level before moving to the omission of increasingly smaller units of sound.

Sing the song BINGO. Call the children's attention to the way they omitted or left out singing letter names.

Teacher: "Yesterday, we played the Hidden Word Game. Do you remember how we played that game?" Give children opportunity to respond.

Teacher: "Yes, I said a long word and we found little words hidden in the long word. Today, we are going to learn a new game called the Guess What Part of the Word is Missing game. In this game, we are going to listen for the hidden word and then try to say the rest of the word without saying the hidden word."

Use the same list of words that was used the previous day to recognize the embedded words.

Teacher: "Say the word <u>catnip</u>. Do you hear the word <u>cat</u> in the word <u>catnip</u>?"

Allow children's response time.

Teacher: "Now say the word <u>catnip</u> again and think about where you heard the word <u>cat</u>. Was it in the beginning or at the end?"

Children respond.

Teacher: "This time, say the word <u>catnip</u> and leave out the part that says <u>cat</u>. Just think <u>cat</u> in your head but don't say it aloud." Teacher places finger in front of her lips for quiet as she says, "Just think. . . . Think or say the first part of the word inside your head and just say the last part."

Children respond.

Teacher: "What part did you leave out?"

Children respond.

Teacher: "Yes, when you leave out the part that says <u>cat</u>, the rest of the word says <u>nip</u>." If children have difficulty, return to asking, "What part did you leave out?"

Teacher: "This time, when you say the word <u>catnip</u>, leave out the part that says <u>nip</u>. Say the first part of the word and just think the last part that says <u>nip</u>."

Children respond.

Teacher: "Yes, when you leave out the part that says <u>nip</u>, the rest of the word says <u>cat</u>." If children have difficulty, return to asking, "What part did you leave out?"

Remember that you are teaching a skill, not testing   Sometimes, it helps to tell the children to just think the rest of the word "inside their heads." Give guidance and support as the children learn to "play" with the words and sounds.

If children are having difficulty, drop back to asking how many syllables or parts did you hear? As they tell you "two," draw lines.

Teacher: "What did this first line (pointing to first straight line) say?"
Children: "<u>Cat</u>."
Teacher: "What did this next line say?"

Children: "Nip."
Teacher: "When we put them together, what did they say?"
Children respond with, "Catnip."

"Say catnip."	"Say cat."	"What part did we leave out?"
catnip	cat	nip
catnip	nip	cat
mailbox	mail	box
mailbox	box	mail
doghouse	house	dog
doghouse	dog	house
into	to	in
into	in	to
outside	side	out
outside	out	side
airplane	air	plane
airplane	plane	air

More Recognition of Missing Units of Sound from Compound Words

Watch your pacing; don't let the session drag. Short periods of practice that move at an interesting pace are most effective for learning.

"Say doghouse."	"Say house."	"What part did we leave out?"
doghouse	house	dog
doghouse	dog	house
mailbox	mail	box
mailbox	box	mail
into	to	in
into	in	to
outside	side	out
outside	out	side
airplane	plane	air
airplane	air	plane
cannot	can	not
cannot	not	can
ramrod	ram	rod
ramrod	rod	ram
girlfriend	girl	friend
girlfriend	friend	girl
boyfriend	boy	friend
boyfriend	friend	boy
fishhook	hook	fish
fishhook	fish	hook
campground	ground	camp

campground	camp	ground
backyard	back	yard
backyard	yard	back

Omitting Units of Sounds from Compound Words

Begin the lesson by singing BINGO.

Teacher: "Today, we are going to play the new word game that we learned yesterday. Do you remember how we played that game? That's right, we left out part of the word. Omit means to leave something out just like we left the letter names out when we sang BINGO.

Give children opportunity to respond.

Teacher: "Yes, the word was omit. If we omit something, we leave it out. When we sang BINGO and left out a letter name, we omitted the name. If I make a peanut butter sandwich and leave out the jelly, you would say that I omitted the jelly. We call this game the Omission Game, meaning we will leave something out."

Sing the song BINGO.

Remind the children that they left out letter names in the song. They thought them in their heads, but didn't sing the letter names out loud.

Ask the children: "Do you remember how they played the Guess What Sound is Missing game with words yesterday?" Allow children to respond and take time to recount how the game was played.

Teacher: "Today, we are going to play the Omission Game. In this game, we are going to omit or leave out part of the word. You will need to listen closely and think part of the word in your head, just like we thought the name of the letters in the song BINGO. When you come to the part of the word that you are going to leave out, just think that part and put your finger in front of your lips as if to say be quiet."

(This exercise has a slightly different approach than was found in the previous exercise. Children are becoming comfortable in playing with words and sounds.)

Review the steps of the game and model the first item.

Teacher: "Say the word cannot." "How many syllables did you hear?" Draw the two lines as the children tell you "two."

Teacher: "What did this first line (pointing to first straight line) say?"

Children: "Can."

Teacher: "What did this next line say?"

Children: "Not."

Teacher: "When we put them together, what did they say?"

Children respond with, "Cannot."

Teacher: "Now say it again, but this time, leave out can. What is left?"

"Say cannot."	"Leave out can." (finger to lips)	"What is left?"
cannot	can	not
cannot	not	can
ramrod	ram	rod
ramrod	rod	ram
girlfriend	girl	friend
girlfriend	friend	girl
boyfriend	boy	friend

boyfriend	friend	boy
childhood	child	hood
childhood	hood	child
friendship	ship	friend
friendship	friend	ship
fishhook	fish	hook
fishhook	hook	fish
mailbox	mail	box
mailbox	box	mail
into	to	in
into	in	to
outside	side	out
outside	out	side
airplane	air	plane
airplane	plane	air

Introducing the Suffix Concept

As we begin this task, take a few minutes to introduce the concept of the suffix. This is what Slingerland referred to as teaching before the fact. Its purpose is to familiarize the children with the suffix concept, which will be carefully retaught and reinforced later during the written spelling procedures in first grade. Teaching this concept employs using an action word, which is then modified. Elicit the modified word from the children using the following technique.

Teacher: "Place your hands beneath your chins and say the word fish. How many times did your chins come down to touch your hands when you said the word fish?" Allow response time. "That's right, it touched your hands one time. How many syllables or parts are there in the word fish?" Allow response time. "Let's try another word. This time your word is fishing. The word fishing tells what someone is doing—Bobby is fishing. How many syllables are there in the word fishing? We used a special kind of syllable called a suffix to change the word fish to the word fishing. It is something that is added to a word to change its meaning just a little bit."

The teacher should then call upon a child to stand in front of the group. She should then ask the rest of the children, "What is (name of child) doing?" The children will respond, "Standing." The teacher will reply, "Yes, I asked (name of child) to stand and now he is standing. We changed the word just a little bit. Place your hands under your chins and tell me how many syllables you hear and feel in the word stand."

Children respond one syllable.

Teacher: "Now say standing. How many syllables to you hear and feel in the word standing?"

Children respond two syllables.

The teacher then asks another child to stand in front of the class and tells the child, "Please jump." She then asks the remainder of the children, "What is (name of child) doing?" Children respond, "(Name of child) is jumping."

The teacher then asks, "What did (name of child) do?" She elicits the word jumped from the group. "Yes, (name of child) jumped. Who can tell me how many syllables they heard and felt in the word jump?"

A child will respond: "I heard and felt one syllable in the word jump."

Teacher: "How many syllables did you hear and feel in the word jumping?"

A child will respond: "I heard and felt two syllables in the word jumping."

Teacher: "How many syllables did you hear and feel in the word <u>jumped</u>?"

A child will respond: "I heard and felt two syllables in the word <u>jumped</u>."

Teacher: "The syllables called suffixes changed the meaning of the word just a little bit."

Other action words that may be used to introduce the suffix concept might include:

skip	skipping	skipped
run	running	runner (one who runs is called a runner)
hop	hopping	hopped
lift	lifting	lifted

Recognizing Embedded Units in Words with Suffixes

<u>The children must have had practice and have been successful in recognition of sound units on page 49, in Recognition of Same Phonemes at the End of Words on page 41, and Introducing the Suffix Concept on page 56 before this exercise is attempted.</u>

Sing the song BINGO. Remind the children that they left out letter names in the song. They thought them in their heads, but didn't sing the letter names out loud.

Ask the children if they remember how they counted the syllables in words. They should review this briefly until you are sure that they are comfortable with that task.

Teacher: "Now, let's play our Hidden Sound game. I will say a long word. There may be a little part of a word hidden in the long word. See if you can hear the little hidden word part."

Teacher's Script:

1. "Say the word <u>fishing</u>."
2. "Did you hear the word <u>fish</u> in the word <u>fishing</u>?"
3. "Was it in the beginning or at the end of the word <u>fishing</u>?"

1.	2.	3.
fishing	fish	beginning
camping	camp	beginning
jumping	jump	beginning
friendly	friend	beginning
runner	run	beginning
laughing	ing	end
broken	broke	beginning
skipping	ing	end
smiling	smile	beginning
lifted	lift	beginning
drawing	draw	beginning

Recognizing Omitted Units of Sound in Words with Suffixes

Sing BINGO (taught previously). Call children's attention to how they omitted or left out singing letter names.

Teacher: "Yesterday, we played the Hidden Word game. Do you remember how we played that game?" Give children opportunity to respond.

Teacher: "Yes, I said a long word and we found little words hidden in the long word. Today, we are going to play the Guess What Part of the Word is Missing game. In this game, we are going to listen for the hidden part of the word and then try to say the rest of the word without saying the hidden part."

"Say fishing."	"Say fish."	"What part did we leave out?"
fishing	fish	ing
fishing	ing	fish
camping	camp	ing
camping	ing	camp
jump	jump	ing
jump	ing	jump
friendly	ly	friend
runner	run	er
runner	er	run
laughing	laugh	ing
skipping	skip	ing
skipping	ing	skip
drawing	draw	ing
drawing	ing	draw
marching	march	ing
marching	ing	march

Omitting Units of Sound from Words with Suffixes

Sing the song BINGO. Remind the children that they omitted or left out letter names in the song. They thought them in their heads, but didn't sing the letter names out loud.

Ask the children if they remember how they played the Guess What Sound Is Missing game with words yesterday. "Today, we are going to play the Omission Game. In this game we are going to omit or leave out part of the word. You will need to listen closely and think part of the word in your head, just like we thought the name of the letters in BINGO. When you come to the part of the word that you are going to leave out, put your finger in front of your lips as if to say be quiet."

Review the steps of the game and model the first item.

Teacher: "Say the word <u>cannot</u>." Allow response time. "Now say it again, but this time, leave out <u>can</u>." "_____ not" (finger to lips)

Teacher's Script:
1. "Say the word <u>runner</u>."
2. "Say <u>runner</u> again, but leave out <u>er</u>." (finger to lips)
3. "What is left?"

---

runner	er	run
laughing	laugh	ing
skipping	skip	ing
skipping	ing	skip
drawing	draw	ing
drawing	ing	draw
marching	march	ing
marching	ing	march
runner	run	er

fishing	ing	fish
finishing	ing	finish
sailor	or	sail
painted	ed	paint

Recognizing Omitted Units of Sound from Words—Syllables

Sing the song BINGO. Remind the children that they left out letter names in the song. They thought them in their heads, but didn't sing the letter names out loud.

Briefly review counting syllables.

Teacher: "Now, let's play our Guess What Sound Is Missing game with syllables in words. Say the word catnip." Children respond.

Teacher: "Now, say cat. What part did we leave out?"

Teacher: "Say the word tennis. Do you hear the syllable ten in the word tennis?" Allow children's response time. "Now say the word tennis again." Allow time for children's response. "This time, say the word ten. What part did we leave out?" Allow children to respond.

Teacher: "If you say the word tennis, but leave out the tenn, the part that is left is is. Let's try some more."

| **_Teacher's Script:_** | | |
"Say candid"	"Say can"	"What part did we leave out?"
candid	can	did
candid	did	can
friendly	friend	ly
friendly	ly	friend
service	ser	vice
service	vice	ser
largest	lar	gest
largest	gest	lar

Recognizing Omitted Units of Sound from Word with Syllables #2

Sing the song BINGO. Remind the children that they left out letter names in the song. They thought them in their heads, but didn't sing the letter names out loud. Ask the children if they remember how they played the Guess Which Syllable Is Missing game yesterday.

Review the recognition of syllables.

Teacher: "Place your hands beneath your chins and say the word simple. How many times did your chins come down to touch your hands when you said the word simple?" Children respond.

Teacher: "That's right, it touched your hand two times. How many syllables or parts are there in the word simple?" Children respond, "Two."

Teacher: "Let's try another word. This time your word is can. How many syllables are there in the word can?" Children respond.

Reinforce with a phrase such as, "Very good!"

Teacher: "Now, let's try playing our Guess What Part is Missing game with syllables in words. Say the word running." Children respond.

Teacher: "Now, say <u>run</u>. What part did we leave out?" Children respond.

Teacher: "If you say the word <u>running</u>, but leave out the /ing/, the part that is left is <u>run</u>. Let's try some more."

Teacher's Script:

"Say <u>eating</u>." "Say <u>ing</u>." "What did we leave out?"

---

eating	ing	eat
wonderful	ful	wonder
motion	mo	tion
motion	tion	mo
teacher	er	teach
table	ble	ta
window	dow	win
*wonderful	won___ful	der
*convention	con___tion	ven
*entertaining	enter___ing	tain

*for very advanced kindergartners and older students

Omitting Units of Sounds from Words—Syllables

Sing the song BINGO. Remind the children that they left out letter names in the song. They thought them in their heads, but didn't sing the letter names out loud.

Ask the children if they remember how they played the Guess What Sound Is Missing game with words yesterday. "Today, we are going to play the Omission Game. In this game, we are going to omit or leave out part of the word. You will need to listen closely and think part of the word in your head, just like we thought the name of the letters in BINGO. When you come to the part of the word that you are going to leave out, put your finger in front of your lips as if to say be quiet."

Review the steps of the game and model the first item.

Teacher: "Say the word <u>cannot</u>. Now say it again, but this time, leave out <u>can</u>."

"____ not" (finger to lips)

Teacher's Script:

"Say <u>letter</u>." "Leave out <u>let</u>." "What is left?"
            (finger to lips)

---

letter	let	ter
finger	fin	ger
review	view	re
welcome	wel	come
lemon	un	lem
yellow	ow	yell
pencil	pen	cil
crayon	cray	on
paper	pa	per
window	dow	win

apple	ple	ap
animal	ani	mal
candle	can	dle
candle	dle	can

Recognizing Embedded Units of Sound in Words—Beginning Phonemes

The objectives of this game is for the children to be able to hold the stimulus words in memory, discriminate between sounds, and recognize the sequence of single sound units—phonemes. Many children have difficulty in holding the correct pronunciation of the word in memory and sequencing sounds.

Research has shown that children are most successful in recognizing the beginning sounds in words. In research completed with third grade students, Lieberman (1974) found that the position of the letters in the word influenced the ability to recognize them. Twice the number of errors occurred when the task required the recognition of the final consonant sound than were found with initial consonant sounds. The most difficulty became apparent when the subjects were required to recognize vowels. Errors in recognizing vowel sounds, regardless of the vowels' position, occurred at twice the frequency of errors in recognizing consonant sounds in any position.

During this initial exercise, only the short /a/ vowel sound will be used. This assists the children in focusing only on the beginning and ending consonant sounds. Note that the first section of the list has only beginning sounds. This is to avoid confusion as we teach a new skill. When the children understand the concept of recognizing the beginning sound, the task will switch to the ending sound. Mixing the beginning and ending sound tasks will follow this. Other vowel sounds may be included after the children become secure in their understanding of the first task.

Teacher: "This game is called the Hidden Sound game. I will say a word. Listen for hidden sounds in the word."

Teacher: "Say the word cat. Did you hear the sound /k/ in the word cat?"

Allow time for children's response.

Teacher: "Where did you hear the sound /k/?"

Children's response.

Continue working with words in the following list. It is suggested that this list be broken into smaller units to use during two to three days of lessons.

Remember, these sound sequencing exercises may be too difficult for younger, less developed children.

Teacher's Script:
1. "Say the word man."
2. "Did you hear the sound /m/ in the word man?"
3. "Where did you hear the sound /m/?"

---

man	/m/	beginning
last	/l/	beginning
tan	/t/	beginning
nap	/n/	beginning
jab	/j/	beginning
raft	/r/	beginning
hasp	/h/	beginning
gab	/g/	beginning

camp	/k/	beginning
sack	/s/	beginning
fan	/f/	beginning

Recognizing Embedded Units of Sound in Words—Ending Phonemes

Be sure that the children are secure in recognizing the beginning consonant sound prior to this exercise in which they will listen for the ending sound. Children with sequencing problems will find this difficult, even though they may be able to hear the sounds.

> Teacher: "Now say the word <u>cat</u> again."
> Children respond.
> "Did you hear the sound /t/ hidden in the word <u>cat</u>?"
> Children respond.
> Teacher: "Where did you hear the sound /t/?"
> Children respond, "At the end of the word."

Teacher's Script:
1. "Say the word <u>gas</u>."
2. "Did you hear the sound /s/ in the word <u>gas</u>?"
3. "Where did you hear the sound /s/?"

---

gas	/s/	end
ham	/m/	end
camp	/p/	end
tack	/k/	end
vast	/t/	end
mat	/t/	end
map	/p/	end
tag	/g/	end
lock	/k/	end

More Recognizing Embedded Units of Sound in Words—Mixed Beginning and Ending Phonemes (Rosner 1993; Slingerland 1969; Slingerland and Murray 1987; Murray 2002)

The object of this game is for the children to be able to hold the stimulus word in memory, discriminate between sounds, recognize the sequence of single sound units—phonemes, omit the sounds pronounced by the teacher, and say the remaining portion of the word (Vail 1992). *Do not initiate this exercise if children are not successful with the two preceding exercises.* In that case, more time needs to be spent on the steps leading up to this stage.

> Teacher: "Today we will play our Hidden Sound game again. I will say a word. See if you can hear a hidden sound in the word. Say the word <u>stop</u>." Children respond by saying the word <u>stop</u>. "Did you hear the sound /s/ in the word <u>stop</u>?"
> Give children opportunity to respond. "Where did you hear the sound /s/?" Children respond.
> Teacher: "Now, say the word <u>stop</u>. Did you hear the sound /p/ in the word <u>stop</u>?"

Children respond. "Where did you hear the sound /p/?" Children respond.
Continue working with words in the following list.

Teacher's Script:
1. "Say the word hat."
2. "Did you hear the sound /h/ in the word hat?"
3. "Where did you hear the sound /h/?"

---

hat	/h/	beginning
fat	/f/	beginning
man	/n/	end
fast	/f/	beginning
fan	/n/	end
mast	/m/	beginning
mast	/t/	end
sash	/s/	beginning
wax	/w/	beginning
trash	/sh/	end
vast	/v/	beginning
trash	/t/	beginning
hasp	/p/	end
glad	/d/	end
plan	/p/	beginning
dirt	/t/	end
mud	/m/	beginning
sand	/d/	end
fig	/f/	beginning
gum	/g/	beginning
fun	/n/	end
stamp	/p/	end
band	/b/	beginning
horn	/h/	beginning
sap	/s/	beginning
sad	/d/	end
cry	/k/	beginning
doll	/d/	beginning
bat	/t/	end
pin	/p/	beginning
rag	/g/	end

Recognizing Number of Sound Units—Number of Phonemes (sounds) in Words

BOX 3 Color cubes, plastic discs or other markers
Prior to beginning this task, be sure that the students have had ample practice in recognizing syllables in words. (Developmentally, children are able to discriminate the larger unit, syllables, before they

are able to discriminate individual phonemes (sounds) (Lieberman 1974). This should be a small group activity and should be continued for several days.

Teacher: "We have been practicing counting the number of words that we heard in sentences. We also practiced hearing the syllables or parts of words. Today, we are going to do something a little different. Listen carefully and see if you can tell me how many little or individual sounds you hear in each word."

Emphasize sounds in the word at: "/a - t/, at." You may also put your hand on your throat as you make the vowel sound /a/, and bring it to your lips and then out from your lips as you make the sound /t/. (You may feel a slight movement or "buzz" on your voice box when making the sound /a/. When forming the sound /t/, the tongue presses against the teeth and the front part of the roof of the mouth, then as it is brought down quickly, a puff of air is expelled from the mouth) (Oliphant 1972).

Teacher: "Let's say the word together, /a - t/, at."
Slowly blend the sounds together. Do not make complete stops between sounds.
"How many sounds do you think that you heard and made?"
Children respond.

Teacher: "Fine, you were really listening. Now, can you use your marker to show me how many sounds are in this word? Put a marker out while you hear and feel your mouth making each sound /a - t/. Great! I see you put out one marker for /a/ and one marker for /t/. You have two markers for the two sounds in the word at" (Lindamood 1975).
No attempt is made to name the letters at this time.

Teacher: "Let's try some more. I'll say the sounds in a word. Then I'll say the word. It may be a real word, it may be a "make believe" word. /i - n/, in. Now, you say the sounds and the word with me. /i - n/, in." Allow time for children's response. "This time, as we say the word, pay attention to how many sounds you hear and feel your mouth making. As you make each sound, place a colored marker in front of you like this" (teacher should model performance).

As you begin this exercise, be sure sounds are those that are easy to see and feel.

Do not attempt to do all of the words in one day. Have several short practice sessions. No attempt is made to name the letters at this time.

/g-o/	go	2	/a-n/	an	2	/u-s/	us	2
/r-a-g/	rag	3	/p-a-n/	pan	3	/s-t-a-g/	stag	4
/t-a-n/	tan	3	/n-a-p/	nap	3	/p-a-th/	path	3
/j-a-b/	jab	3	/e-n-d/	end	3	/r-a-f-t/	raft	4
/b-u-g/	bug	3	/n-u-n/	nun	3	/b-u-n-t/	bunt	4
/m-u-d/	mud	3	/h-u-g/	hug	3	/b-u-n-k/	bunk	4
/l-u-g/	lug	3	/r-u-n/	run	3	/l-u-n-ch/	lunch	5
/d-u-g/	dug	3	/s-l-u-g/	slug	4	/b-u-n-ch/	bunch	4
/s-t-u-n	/stun	4	/ch-u-g/	chug	3	/s-p-o-t/	spot	4
/h-o-t/	hot	3	/j-o-g/	jog	3	/t-r-o-t/	trot	4
/r-o-d/	rod	3	/m-o-p/	mop	3	/t-r-o-d/	trod	4
/c-o-p/	cop	3	/h-o-p/	hop	3	/s-t-o-p/	stop	4
/g-a-s/	gas	3	/h-a-g/	hag	3	/p-a-n-t/	pant	4
/w-a-g/	wag	3	/s-a-g/	sag	3	/s-t-a-n-d/	stand	5
/f-l-a-g/	flag	4	/b-r-a-g/	brag	4	/d-a-d/	dad	3
/m-a-d/	mad	3	/h-a-d/	had	3	/p-a-d/	pad	3

/s-a-d/	sad	3	/g-l-a-d/	glad	4	/b-r-a-t/	brat	4
/ch-a-t/	chat	3	/f-l-a-t/	flat	4	/b-r-a-d/	brad	4
/j-i-g/	jig	3	/p-i-g/	pig	3	/w-i-g/	wig	3
/z-i-g/	zig	3	/b-r-i-g/	brig	4	/b-i-b/	bib	3
/b-a-b/	bab	3	/l-i-ck/	lick	3	/s-i-ck/	sick	3
/c-a-n/	can	3	/b-a-g/	bag	3	/s-p-a-n/	span	4

Recognizing Number of Sound Units—Number of Phonemes (Sounds) in Words—More Practice

The ability to hear individual phonemes (sounds) may be too difficult for some students at this time. It should not be attempted unless the children have shown that they are able to hear individual phonemes. Working with small groups of children will enable you to carefully observe the developmental readiness for this activity.

Words have been provided for several days' lessons. No attempt is made to name the letters at this time.

/I/	I	1	/a-m/	am	2	/a-b/	ab	2
/b-a/	ba	2	/i-t/	it	2	/a-t/	at	2
/s-a-d/	sad	3	/s-i-t/	sit	3	/c-a-t/	cat	3
/m-a-d/	mad	3	/b-a-t/	bat	3	/b-a-g/	bag	3
/r-a-g/	rag	3	/t-a-b/	tab	3	/r-a-t/	rat	3
/f-a-b/	fab	3	/p-o/	po	2	/o-p/	op	2
/i- p/	ip	2	/p-i-p/	pip	3	/p-o-p/	pop	3
/t-i-s/	tis	3	/f-i-z/	fiz	3	/b-a-m/	bam	3
/t-o/	to	2	/f-i/	fi	2	/h/a/m/	ham	3
/h-a-t/	hat	3	/b-i-v/	biv	3	/b-o-t/	bot	3
/s-a-m/	sam	3	/s-a-p/	sap	3	/a-b/	ab	2
/a-sh/	ash	2	/m-a-p/	map	3	/g-a-p/	gap	3
/l-a-p/	lap	3	/m-ay/	may	2	/p-a-n/	pan	3
/c-o-b/	cob	3	/h-i-t/	hit	3	/r-i-b/	rib	3
/c-r-i-b/	crib	4	/d-u-s-t/	dust	4	/h-u-t/	hut	3
/b-u-d/	bud	3	/u-s/	us	2	/j-u-t/	jut	3
/b-i-t/	bit	3	/l-a-p/	lap	3	/z-i-p/	zip	3
/l-i-s-t/	list	4	/h-e-n/	hen	3	/t-e-n-t/	tent	4

Recognizing and Manipulating Individual Sound Units—Phonemes (Lindamood and Lindamood 1984)

Today, this individual sound manipulation exercise may be introduced (Lindamood and Lindamood 1984).

Teacher: "Listen carefully, and tell me how many sounds I am making. /h/ /h/"

Pause for children to respond.

Teacher: "Show me, with your colored markers, how many sounds I made."

Children respond by placing two of the same colored markers.

Teacher: "Good! These markers say /h/ - /h/. We will use the same color because they are making the same sound. Now, listen closely because I may change the sounds that I say. Place your markers to show me the sounds that you hear. /h/ - /t/." (pause)

"How many sounds did you hear? Were they the same sound or did I make two different sounds?" (Pause for response.)

"You can show me that you heard two different sounds by placing two different colored markers." (Demonstrate as the children follow your procedure.)

"First I said /h/. (Place marker.) Then I said /t/." (Place marker.)

Repeat while pointing at the markers: "/h/ - /t/."

"Now, I am going to change it. Listen carefully. /h/ - /b/ How many sounds did you hear?" (Pause for response.)

"Which sound did I change, the first sound or the second sound?" (Pause for response.)

"Yes, I changed the second sound, so I must change my second marker."

Demonstrate and have the children manipulate their markers.

"Listen carefully. Show me /h/ - /t/ - /h/. How many sounds did you hear?"

Children respond.

"Yes, this time we added a sound. It was the same sound as the one in the beginning, so we will use the same colored marker." (Demonstrate.)

"This time, show me /s/."

Continue guiding the children through manipulation of markers until they seem secure in the process. Always reinforce by asking, "How many sounds did you hear? Which sound did I change (add or take away)?"

Note: Specific colors are not assigned to specific sounds. However, in any set, the same color must be used for a repeated sound.

Have children clear markers away before beginning a new set. The three asterisks *** divide the sets.

Show me:

/s/ /m/	two different colored markers
/s/ /s/	retain first marker, change second marker to same color as first
/s/ /f/	two different colored markers (show children to retain the first marker and change the last)
***	clear working space
/b/ /b/	two same colored markers
/b/ /a/	change second marker
/b/ /a/ /t/	add third colored marker
/b/ /a/ /b/	change third marker to match first
/b/ /a/ /g/	change third marker to a new color
/b/ /a/	retain first and second markers
/a/	children should retain second marker
/a/ /m/	retain first marker, add new color for second marker
/m/ /a/	reverse positions of markers
/m/ /a/ /m/	add third marker which is the same color as the first
***	clear working space
/p/ /p/	two same colored markers
/p/ /t/	retain first marker, add second different colored marker
/t/	remove first marker, retain second marker
/t/ /i/	retain first marker, add second different colored marker

/t/ /i/ /p/   retain first and second marker, add third different colored marker
/t/ /i/ /p/ /s/   retain first, second and third marker, add fourth different colored marker
/i/ /p/ /s/   remove first colored marker, retain second, third and fourth markers

Continue guiding the children through manipulation of markers until they seem secure in the process. This will probably take several days. Always reinforce by asking, "How many sounds did you hear? Which sound (first, middle, or last) did I change (add or take away)?"

Show me:

/b/ /b/   two same colored markers
/h/ /b/   change first marker, retain second marker
/k/ /t/   two different colored markers
/t/ /t/   change first marker to match second marker

***   clear working space

Show me:

/a/   one colored marker
/t/ /a/   place new first marker, retain previous marker as second marker
/t/ /a/ /t/   retain first and second markers, add third marker to match first
/t/ /a/ /m/ retain first and second markers, change last marker
/h/ /a/ /m/ change first marker, retain second and third markers
/h/ /i/ /m/ retain first and third markers, change middle marker
/h/ /i/ /t/   retain first and second markers, change last marker
/b/ /i/ /t/   change first marker, retain second and third markers
/b/ /i/ /g/   change last marker
/b/ /a/ /g/   change middle marker
/b/ /a/ /t/   change last marker
/s/ /a/ /t/   change first marker
/s/ /i/ /t/   change middle marker
/s/ /i/ /m/   change last marker
/d/ /i/ /m/   change first marker
/d/ /i/ /d/   change last marker
/d/ /i/ /g/   change last marker
/f/ /i/ /g/   change first marker

More Recognizing and Manipulating Individual Sound Units—Phonemes

Review previously taught activities in manipulating colored markers to represent individual sound units (phonemes). Continue guiding the children through manipulation of markers until they seem secure in the process.

Show me:

/k/ /k/   two same colored markers
/k/ /m/   change last marker
/k/ /t/   change last marker
/t/ /t/   change first marker
/t/ /a/ /t/   retain first and third marker, insert different colored second marker
/t/ /a/ /g/   change last marker

/t/ /a/ /m/   change last marker
/h/ /a/ /m/   change first marker
/h/ /i/ /m/   change middle marker

***   clear working space

When children seem secure in representing sounds as you say individual phonemes, proceed to saying sounds as one unit.

Show me:

/a/ (short vowel sound)	one colored marker
/i/ (short vowel sound)	one colored marker (change color)
/u/ (short vowel sound)	one colored marker (change color)
/la/ (short vowel sound)	two different colored markers
/pa/ (short vowel sound)	change first marker
/ma/(short vowel sound)	change first marker
/ta/ (short vowel sound)	change first marker
/tu/ (short vowel sound)	change second marker
/ut/ (short vowel sound)	reverse markers

Recognizing Omitted Units of Sounds from Words—Phonemes

The objective of this lesson is for the children to be able to hold the stimulus word in memory, discriminate between sounds, and recognize the sequence of single sound units—phonemes.

Sing the song BINGO. Remind the children that they left out or omitted the letter names in the song. They thought them in their heads, but didn't sing the letter names out loud.

Teacher: "Do you remember how we played the game? I said a word and you found the hidden sound. Sometimes we want to listen for the individual little sounds. Let's try it now."
Teacher: "Say the word bag. Do you hear the sound /b/ in the word bag?"
Children respond.
Teacher: "Now say the sounds /ag/. What sound was missing? What sound did we leave out?"
Give children opportunity to respond.
Teacher: "Yes, this time we couldn't hear the sound /b/. If you say the word bag, but leave out the /b/, the part that is left is /ag/. Let's try some more."

Remember, this exercise may be too difficult for younger, less developed children.

"Say ham."	"Say am."	"What sound did we leave out?"
ham	/am/	/h/
sam	/am	/s/
tam	/am/	/t/
ram	/am/	/r/
say	/ay/	/s/
day	/ay/	/d/
ray	/ay/	/r/
fay	/ay/	/f/
may	/ay/	/m/
mat	/at/	/m/
sat	/at/	/s/

hat	/at/	/h/
fat	/at/	/f/
rat	/at/	/r/
pat	/at/	/p/
vat	/at/	/v/
sit	/it/	/s/
hit	/it/	/h/
mitt	/it/	/m/
fit	/it/	/f/
bit	/it/	/b/
pit	/it/	/p/
nag	/ag/	/n/
fox	/ox/	/f/
hat	/at/	/h/
beef	/bee/	/f/
up	/p/	/u/
cup	/cu/	/p/
fish	/fi/	/sh/
ham	/am/	/h/
sam	/am/	/s/
tam	/am/	/t/
ram	/am/	/r/
say	/ay/	/s/
day	/ay/	/d/
ray	/ay/	/r/
fay	/ay/	/f/
may	/ay/	/m/
mat	/at/	/m/
sat	/at/	/s/
man	/an/	/m/
bat	/at/	/b/

Sequencing and Omitting Units of Sounds from Words—Phonemes

Sing the song BINGO. Remind the children that they left out letter names in the song. They thought them in their heads, but didn't sing the letter names out loud.

Ask the children if they remember how they played the Guess What Sound is Missing game with words yesterday. "Today, we are going to play the Omission Game. Remember, in this game we are going to omit or leave out part of the word. You will need to listen closely and think part of the word in your head, just like we thought the name of the letters in BINGO. When you come to the part of the word that you are going to leave out, put your finger in front of your lips as if to say be quiet."

Review the steps of the game and model the first item.

Teacher: "Say the word can. Are you able to say the word can without using the /k/ sound? Let's try. First, say the word can. Now say it again, but this time, leave out /k/." (Give sound, not letter name). "Very good! We are going to play the Omission Game with the little sounds in words. I will say a word. Then, we will see if we can say it while just thinking some sounds."

Teacher's Script:

1. "Say the word____."
2. "Now say it again, but this time, leave out the /__ /." (Give sound, not letter name)

Say word	Leave out	Correct Response
can	/k/	/an/
	(finger to lips)	
in	i/	/n/
up	/p/	/u/
cup	/k/	/up/
fish	/f/	/ish/
ham	/am/	/h/
sam	/am/	/s/
tam	/t/	/am/
ram	/am/	/r/
hat	/at/	/h/
fat	/f/	/at/
rat	/at/	/r/
fat	/at/	/f/
rat	/r/	/at/
bay	/b/	/ay/
pat	/p/	/at/
vat	/v/	/at/
sit	/it/	/s/
hit	/it/	/h/
mitt	/it/	/m/
fit	/it/	/f/
bit	/it/	/b/
pit	/it/	/p/
nag	/ag/	/n/
fox	/ox/	/f/
hat	/at/	/h/
cup	/cu/	/p/
fish	/fi/	/sh/
mast	/ast/	/m/
last	/ast/	/l/
fast	/ast/	/f/
cast	/ast/	/k/
beef	/bee/	/f/
mast	/m/	/ast/
last	/l/	/ast/
fast	/f/	/ast/
cast	/ast/	/k/
stop	/st/	/op/
bat	/at/	/b/
pat	/p/	/at/

More Advanced Recognition of the Number of Individual Sound Units within Words

During the earlier exercise, you carefully made the sounds in slow motion before pronouncing the word at a normal speed. Now, some children will be ready to hear a word and indicate the number of sounds. Again, you should pronounce the word clearly, but not separate sounds. Children should hold up fingers or move colored markers to tell how many sounds they hear.

rib 3	bug 3	hit 3	it 2	rug 3
at 2	hut 3	bag 3	tan 3	sag 3
bad 3	van 3	an 2	lap 3	bat 3
lap 3	as 2	jab 3	ham 3	I 1
lamp 4	raft 4	mad 3	back 3	mad 3

If this lesson is too advanced for the group, go back to giving the individual sounds before pronouncing the word. Keep in mind that the ability to hear individual phonemes is influenced by development. Don't attempt to force a skill that the children are not ready to acquire.

Recognizing and Manipulating Individual Sound Units within Words

Take a few minutes to review use of markers in representing sound sequences.

Show me:

/a/ /g/"	two different colored markers
/b/ /a/ /g/	add different colored first marker
/h/ /a/ /g/	change first marker
/h/ /i/ /g/	change middle marker

Teacher: "Now, we are going to make words with our markers."

Show me:

tat	2 same colored markers with a different colored marker in middle

Repeat word after children have arranged markers.

Teacher: "Let's say our word together: tat."

Continue in same manner, always having children repeat the word when it is completed.

Show me:

tam	change last marker
ham	change first marker
him	change middle marker
hit	change last marker
bit	change first marker
big	change last marker
bag	change middle marker
bat	change last marker
sat	change first marker
sit	change middle marker
sim	change last marker

dim	change first marker
dig	change last marker
did	change last marker
fig	change first and last markers
fit	change last marker
fan	change middle and last markers

LEARNING TO NAME AND FORM LETTERS OF THE ALPHABET: THE KINDERGARTEN ADAPTATION OF THE SLINGERLAND SIMULTANEOUS MULTISENSORY APPROACH

The Slingerland simultaneous multisensory approach for teaching children to recognize and form alphabet letters (graphemes) has proven to be effective for both children with dyslexia and/or dysgraphia, as well as for the majority of children who do not have learning disabilities. Many school districts have used this instructional approach throughout their districts. The techniques and strategies of the approach are discussed briefly here. The reader is encouraged to seek more in-depth instruction from Slingerland teacher-education classes taught throughout the United States by the Slingerland Institute for Literacy or by referring to the following publications:

Learning to Use Manuscript Handwriting, Slingerland and Aho 1985a

Masters for Learning to Use Manuscript Handwriting, Slingerland and Aho 1985b

Learning to Use Cursive Handwriting, Slingerland and Aho 1985c

Masters for Learning to Use Cursive Handwriting, Slingerland and Aho 1985d

A Multi-Sensory Approach to Language Arts for Specific Language Disability Children: A Guide for Primary Teachers, (Textbook I), Slingerland 1996

A Multi-Sensory Approach to Language Arts for Specific Language Disability Children: A Guide for Elementary Teachers, (Textbook III), Slingerland 1994

The reader might ask, "Why is handwriting being introduced in the middle of phonemic awareness?" This is being done because the kinesthetic/motor memory of the formation of letters assists the child to learn and recall the names and sounds of letters. With traditional instruction, approximately 20% of children continue to have difficulty in associating sounds and the corresponding graphic symbols. The kinesthetic (automatic memory of movement) used in forming the letters has proven effective in developing these associations for high-risk children. The child who is not at high risk for a language disability also learns better with this instruction.

The Slingerland Approach uses simultaneous multisensory strategies in which the child:

- sees the letter.
- hears the name of the letter.
- feels the sequence of movements in his arm as he traces a large pattern.
- feels the sequence of movements in his speech organs as he says the letter name.

These strategies not only help develop letter recognition, but also help children in developing writing skills without placing performance demands that they are physically unready to fulfill.

Single stroke manuscript (printing) letter formations assist students in developing automatic letter formation skills. It is important to begin with the lower case letters rather than with capitals or uppercase letters. The child must recognize lower case letters instantly and automatically when reading words. Whenever uppercase letters are used, there is a slight pause as additional conceptual information is being provided to the brain, such as a new sentence, a proper name, an abbreviation, or a code. Learning the uppercase letters develops easily after the lower case letters are mastered.

Introduction to Names and Formations of Letters

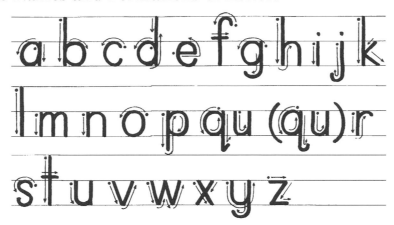

Recognizing and Naming Letters of the Alphabet

Keyword Cards

Keyword patterns suggested by Slingerland are:

a-apple b-ball c-cake d-duck, e-elephant, f-fish, g-goat, h-house, i-inch, j-jam, k-kite, l-lamp, m-mittens, n-nest, o-olives, p-pig, qu-queen, r-rug, s-sun, t-turtle, u-umbrella, v-vase, w-wagon, x-box, y-yarn, z-zebra, ck-Jack, ch-chair, th-this (voiced), th-thimble (unvoiced), wh-wheel.

As the lesson begins, hold up a keyword card with a large lower-case letter. In later lessons, it will be helpful if the card also contains a carefully chosen keyword that begins with the sound of the letter. (Both keyword and alphabet cards can be made or purchased.)[3]

Tell the children the name of this letter. The children in the group repeat the name. Each child is then given an individual opportunity to name the letter, as you hold the card in front of him or her. Thus, the child sees the letter (visual), hears its name (auditory), and receives kinesthetic-motor reinforcement in the speech organs when repeating the name. If the child hesitates and has difficulty retrieving the name, simply say the name of the letter and let the child repeat it. Remember, this is teaching, not testing.

Learning to Form the Letters

When the children are familiar with the name of the letter, write a 12- to 15-inch letter on the board, naming the letter as it is formed. A child is given the opportunity to trace the letter while saying the letter name. At this point, the kinesthetic-motor movements in the arm are added to the Auditory-Visual-Kinesthetic-Motor integrations. It is often useful to assist the child. Hold the child's hand and guide it through the tracing. It is important for the child to feel the sequence of movement while tracing the letter. He will be unable to feel this sequence if he slows down and draws the letter in an effort to be perfect. At the kindergarten and first grade level, it is not suggested to begin by pointing out the lines during the teaching of the <u>first seven or eight letters</u> as this just complicates the task and encourages "drawing" rather than printing. After the child has the "feel" of the rhythm of writing, it is easier to introduce the lines and use lines in teaching new letters. Of course, you should always use proper size relationships while forming patterns. (I have had experience teaching children both with and without lines. In the beginning, young children were better able to develop the automatic movements needed to form the letters when lines were not used during introduction.)

Talking Through the Formation of Letters

Now you are ready to "talk though the formation" of the letter. This is an example of teaching through the intellect. The children are being taught a strategy for remembering by knowing how to talk themselves through the formation rather than guessing or relying on memory or gimmicks.

Example of "talking through the formation:"

Teacher: "The letter h begins with a tall stem down, back up, around and down—h."

Then have the children help you talk through the formation while using their arms to form the letter in the air.

"The arms are extended with the elbows comfortably bent, the hands about at the same level as the top of the head to allow for the downward stroke of the tall letters and at eye level for the shorter letters. This allows for easy swings from the shoulder blades. The two first fingers held together are used in place of a pencil" (Slingerland 1996, p. 44).

Then place several letters on the board.

Several children trace the letters while saying their names.

Other children in the group will form the letter with their arm swing (as described above) while simultaneously saying the letter name.

Letter Formations—Tracing Large Patterns

Large permanent patterns for tracing are given to each child in the group. These patterns may be made on 9x12 newsprint or sturdier construction paper. A bit of texture can be added by placing a piece of fine window screen under the paper, then writing the letter with wax crayon. Sandpaper is not used as it may be rough on the fingertips and we do not want to loose the rhythm (memory of movement) of the tracing.

Children will use their first two fingers in place of a pencil for tracing over the pattern. Care should be taken that they continue to use their arm swing from the shoulder (not just moving fingers) and say the name each time they trace the letter. Say the name of the letter to maintain the rhythm. Do not let children resort to drawing instead of writing. Remember that the goal is to develop the automatic memory of sequential movements for forming the letter.

When the children are able to move their arms freely, they are ready to use the <u>unsharpened</u> ends of their pencils. Give children guidance in the proper manner of holding a pencil. The larger, primary pencils should be used. The hexagon shaped primary pencils are easier for small hands to hold. Pencils should not have erasers.

Several copies of the permanent pattern may be laminated and placed at an activity center for children to "choose" to trace with a crayon or grease pencil.

Be aware of those children who elect to choose this activity and those who show no interest in practicing. This is another clue regarding readiness. If the child is not neurologically ready, the task consumes too much energy and is not enjoyable (see Section II).

Reinforcing Letter Formations—Rainbowing Letters[4]

Children will be rainbowing letters, in other words, tracing the letter with various colored crayons or markers, to make a rainbow-colored letter.

Give children letter patterns that have a small picture of the keyword in the upper right-hand corner.

The activity begins with children forming a letter in the air with an arm swing. This is repeated three times.

Children can trace the letters with their two fingers and then "rainbow" letters by using different colored crayons. As the children trace, they should always say the name of the letter. This page may be collected in individual pupil books or sent home to share with parents.

Additional Reinforcing Activities

While holding a card in front of a child's eyes to block her view, guide the child's arm in forming a letter on the chalk or white board. The child should then try to name the letter. If she has difficulty, guide her

Child rainbowing letter with different colors to develop automatic feel of the letter's formation.

hand in tracing over the letter. If the child is still unable to name the letter, talk through the formation as you guide her arm. As a last resort:

- you should talk through the formation as you guide the child's arm, ending up with pronouncing the name of the letter. Obviously, this procedure should not be done until you feel fairly sure the kinesthetic feel of the letter is secure.
- You may use your fingers to write a large letter on the child's back. The child then names the letter. If the child has difficulty, repeat the formation. If it is still unknown, guide the child's arm through the movement.
- Other fun ways to reinforce the recognition of the letter formation include writing large letters in sand or finger paint.
- Beans or macaroni can be glued on patterns to form letters.
- Letters can also be formed using play dough or clay; however, that will not reinforce the automatic memory of movements.

Further Development of Handwriting Skills

Many children of kindergarten age are not neurologically ready to proceed further with handwriting. Carefully evaluate each individual child's apparent development before proceeding further. The technique that should be used with the group that is ready involves working with large patterns, preferably on a white or black board.

- Make a large letter on the board. The child should stand in front of the pattern and form the letter in the air with a full arm swing as he says the name of the letter. This should be repeated three times.

- Then the child will trace over your pattern while saying the name of the letter. Care should be taken that he keeps the same rhythm and does not slow down to draw the letter. This should also be repeated three times.
- The child then moves to the right and forms a copy of the letter on the board.

Trace, Copy, and Write Letters from Memory

If the previous activity was a successful experience, you may gradually reduce the size of the letters. The children who are ready may now be moved down to folded newsprint, using the "trace, copy, and write from memory" techniques as described by Slingerland and Aho (Slingerland 1971; Slingerland and Aho 1985).

DEVELOPING SKILL IN GRAPHEME-PHONEME ASSOCIATION: THE KINDERGARTEN ADAPTATION OF THE SLINGERLAND SIMULTANEOUS MULTISENSORY APPROACH

Associating Sounds with Alphabet Letters

When the name has been attached to a letter form, the child is ready to associate its sound. The Slingerland Multisensory Approach, using a keyword beginning with a corresponding letter (grapheme) and sound (phoneme), assists the child in making these associations.

Introduction of Keywords and Sounds

Please note: an underlined letter (h) indicates that the name is to be pronounced. When a letter is set aside by two slashes (/h/), the sound is to be given.

Hold the keyword card in front of the students and tell them the letter's name while pointing to the letter.

Children learning to form letters.

While pointing to the picture of the keyword, the keyword is named.

Clearly give the beginning sound while pointing to the first letter in the word below the picture.

Demonstrate for the pupils: "This is the way we tell about this letter." Form the letter in the air while saying the name, then give the keyword, and finally give the sound. Care should be taken not to add a vowel sound to a consonant. "h - house - /h/"

Then invite the pupils to practice with you. After several group practices, children are given the opportunity to perform individually.

The child traces the letter or forms the letter in the air, while saying the name "h."

After completing the formation of the letter, the child names the keyword "house," and finally, the child gives the sound /h/.

Thus the pattern: "h - house - /h/"

Suggested Sequence for Teaching Grapheme-Phoneme Association

A suggested sequence for teaching grapheme-phoneme association is as follows. Usually, the first letter taught is h. It is chosen due to the ease with which children can hear and reproduce the sound /h/. The sound of the letter l is more difficult and should not be the first letter introduced in the primary grades.

The short sounds of vowels are taught before the other vowel sounds due to their single spelling. Delay teaching long vowel sounds until later due to spelling complexity.

1. h	2. t	3. l	4. f	5. b
6. c	7. a	8. k	9. ck	10. g
11. s	12. d	13. i	14. j	15. m
16. r	17. n	18. p	19. u	20. y
21. w	22. o	23. v	24. x	25. z
26. ch	27. sh	28. wh	29. th (voiced)	
30. th (voiceless)	31. e			

The formation of the e may be taught earlier; however, the short e sound is very hard for kindergarten and first grade children to hear. They often confuse it with the short i sound. Usually, it is better to wait until auditory discrimination skills are further developed.

Special Introduction for Teaching Vowels

As described by Beth Slingerland in her *Guide for Primary Teachers* (1996) in the Slingerland Approach, the first vowel taught is the short a. It is important that teachers realize that this procedure is teaching more than just the name and sound of this vowel. It is developing the understanding or concept of vowels and the way that vowels make our spelling possible.

The procedure begins as it did with teaching consonants. Show the wall card and tell the children the name of the vowel. Explain that the letter "a is called a vowel and that a vowel sound causes people to do something special every time a word is pronounced" (Slingerland 1971, 1996, p. 66).

Children are asked to "listen and to think to see if they can discover the special reason for vowel sounds."

Teacher: "If I were to play ball with you, I might tell you to get the ball while I get the bt. You get the ball while I get the bt" (Slingerland 1971, 1996, p. 66).

The children are very quick to point out the teacher's mispronunciation of the word bat. In my own experience, one of the first children to correct my mispronunciation was a limited English speaker.

Teacher: "You were really listening and thinking. What did I fail to do that would have helped me say the word <u>bat</u>? bt - bat, bt - bat."

> Some child will discover that the throat must open before the word can be spoken correctly and understandably. Children may discover for themselves the short sound of <u>a</u>, but the teacher tells and shows how the throat opens and has the children experiment with this feeling when they repeat words named by the teacher; e.g., lag, tam, pad, rag, fat, sap, wham, ran, van, ham. This is the time for the vowel concept to be understood. (Slingerland 1971, 1996, pp. 66-67)

When children understand the concept that every syllable has to have a vowel in order to blend the sounds together, the later teaching of multisyllabic words is quite easy. It is exciting to see the eyes of a 6-year-old light up when the teacher places the first multisyllabic word on the board. Often, without further guidance from the teacher, a child will volunteer that the word has two or three parts because he sees two or three vowels. My favorite word to use in this introduction is "fantastic" because I can easily use it in a sentence to tell the children how fantastic they are as students. This success begins with the manner in which the vowel concept is introduced and reinforced. Children enjoy being able to work out problems for themselves. You must provide them with the skills for developing this independence. Then give the children the opportunity and the quiet time to think.

Clarifying and Strengthening Grapheme–Phoneme Association

Recognition of the sounds can be strengthened through the following activities.

Association from Auditory Stimulus—"Auditory Cards"

As children learn new letters, letter cards should be added to your hand pack, the keyword card should be placed on the wall, and a small letter card should also be placed on a card chart.

Daily, conduct a short card drill from both auditory and visual stimuli.

The steps for the auditory card drill are as follows.
As this begins, <u>do not show the alphabet card</u>.
Teacher: "What says /h/ as in house?"
Child: "<u>h</u> - house - /h/" while forming the letter in the air with a full arm swing.

At this point, expose the letter card, and the group repeats "<u>h</u> - house - /h/ while forming the letter in the air with a full arm swing.

As the children become familiar with associating the sound (phoneme) with the letter (grapheme), you may shorten your question to, "What says /h/?" and finally to just making the sound "/h/."

Using eye contact rather than constantly calling the children's names to indicate whose turn it is to answer assists with the pacing of the lesson, keeping it brief and effective. Good pacing is effective in promoting learning and is greatly appreciated by the children. One of the hardest things that we learn as teachers and parents is not to "talk too much."

Association from Visual Stimulus—"Visual Cards"

This drill is also done on a daily basis. It is just the opposite of the Auditory Card Drill.
In this drill, <u>begin by exposing</u> the card. Call upon a child to tell you about the card.
Child: "<u>h</u> - house - /h/" while forming the letter in the air with a full arm swing.
The group repeats "<u>h</u> - house - /h/" while forming the letter in the air with a full arm swing.

Observing Movement of Lips, Tongue, and Teeth during Pronunciation of Sounds

Ask the children to watch your mouth carefully as words beginning with the featured sound are spoken. (There may be a need to further describe the movement of the tongue, teeth, or lips in making the sounds. For assistance with this, refer to the wonderful resource book, *Alphabet Alchemy: The Magic of Transforming Sounds into Letters* by Genevieve Oliphant.)

FOLDER 24 Recognizing Initial Sounds of Naming Words

Hold up a card with a picture of an item whose name begins with the featured sound.

A child is called upon to name the picture. Example: <u>mat</u>

Teacher: "What do you hear and feel when you begin to say (name of picture)?"
The child gives the sound /m/.
Teacher: "Tell me about that sound."
The child then follows the pattern "(<u>letter name while forming in the air</u>) - (keyword) - /sound/," "<u>m</u> - mittens - /m/." Hand the card to the child to place under the correct letter on a pocket chart.

Phoneme-Grapheme Association and Discrimination of Letters

When two or more letters have been introduced, pictures may be used. After the child has named the word, given the sound, and then followed the pattern "<u>letter name while forming in the air</u> - keyword - /sound/," the child places the card under the correct letter on the pocket chart.

Sound of the Day

Children bring in objects or pictures that begin with the featured sound.

Make a Sound Book

Have children locate pictures in catalogues and magazines that begin with the identified sounds. Paste pictures on pages labeled with designated letter.

Children playing Spin the Bottle with sounds.

FOLDER 24 Picture Card Sound Discrimination

Place two cards with designated letters on a card chart. Children take turns drawing picture cards from a pack of picture cards, naming the picture, giving its beginning sound, naming the letter that makes the beginning sound, and placing the picture cards under the correct letter.

FOLDER 24 Picture Card Sound Discrimination Game

Give each child one or two letter cards. Children take turns drawing cards from a pack of picture cards, naming the picture, giving its beginning sound, naming the letter that makes this sound, and placing it with the correct letter card. The child with the most picture cards using their letter card sounds wins the game.

FOLDER 24 Matching Picture and Letter Card Game

Place several cards with printed letters and picture cards in two stacks. Two children turn up the top cards in each stack at the same time. If a letter card and a card with a picture beginning with the corresponding sound turn up at the same time, the player slaps the table. The first player to slap the table moves these cards into his collection. The child who collects the most cards wins.

Spin the Bottle with Sounds

Children name a word that begins with the sound of the designated letter sound when the spun bottle points to them. If successful, the child takes a turn to spin the bottle. If unable to name a word, the turn reverts to the previous player. Reinforce visually by displaying the letter card.

Bean Bag Toss #1

Secure three large round ice-cream cartons. Place a printed letter on the outside. A child tosses a beanbag into the carton. The child then names a word that begins with the letter printed on the carton.

Bean Bag Toss #2

Name a letter as you toss the bean bag to the child. The child must name a word that begins with that sound before tossing the bean bag back or to another child. This child also names a word beginning with the same sound. Reinforce visually by displaying the letter card.

Bean Bag Toss #3

A variation of the preceding game that allows the child who gave the correct sound to name a new letter. Again, reinforce visually by displaying the letter card.

Hopscotch

Use chalk to draw hopscotch on the sidewalk. Place a letter in each box. Children must give the name of the word that begins with the letter sound that corresponds with the one written in the box when they land in the box.

Clapping to Specified Beginning Sound in Words

Ask children to listen for a specified sound. Reinforce visually by displaying the letter card. Pronounce the group of words. Children clap when they hear words beginning with the specified sound.

Listening for Specified Sounds in a Story

Ask children to listen for words beginning with a specified sound and raise "thumbs up" when they hear that sound. Reinforce the learning visually by displaying the corresponding letter card.

Clapping to Specified Ending Sounds in Words

Pronounce a list of words. Children clap when they hear words ending in the specified sound. Again, reinforce visually by showing the corresponding letter card.

Associating Graphemes with Phonemes within Written Words

Occasionally, after the children have become quite familiar with several letters and their sound-symbol (phoneme-grapheme) association, the following game can be played. This is not reading, but again, is a preparation that assists children in linking symbols with sounds.

Print several words on the board that begin with letters that the children have been taught.

Example:

    hand
    top
    man
    land

Teacher: "Who can find thc word <u>top</u>?"

A child places a marker under the word.

If the child is correct, ask the child how he knew it said <u>top</u>. Through discussion, it is brought out that the word begins with a <u>t</u> and the child heard you begin the word with the sound /t/. If the child has difficulty, guide him in listening for the beginning sound and then looking at the beginning letter of the first word.

Teacher: "Does this word begin with the sound /t/?"

The child will respond. If the child thinks the first word does begin with a /t/, ask her to tell you, "What says /t/ as in <u>turtle</u>?" The child will respond with the pattern that she has been taught. Thus, you will guide her to success in finding the correct word.

(At this point, it is unusual for the child not to find the correct word at first. If this happens, you should check carefully to be sure that the teaching pace has not been rushed ahead of the children's maturational learning pace.)

This activity can then continue with recognizing other words beginning with sounds the children have been taught.

DEVELOPING SKILL IN GRAPHEME-PHONEME ASSOCIATIONS (AUDITORY APPROACH) BEGINNING ENCODING: THE KINDERGARTEN ADAPTATION OF THE SLINGERLAND SIMULTANEOUS MULTISENSORY APPROACH

The steps for encoding, or combining sounds that have been heard into words, will be discussed briefly in this book. It is strongly suggested that the reader refer to *A Multi-Sensory Approach to Language Arts for Specific Language Disability Children: A Guide for Primary Teachers* by Beth H. Slingerland for detailed instructions, teaching strategies, and lesson plans that include encoding. The use of these techniques is greatly facilitated by teacher-education classes, which are available through the Slingerland Institute for Literacy.

When the consonants <u>h</u>, <u>l</u>, <u>b</u>, <u>t</u>, <u>f</u>, <u>c</u>, <u>r</u>, <u>m</u>, and the short vowel <u>a</u> have been taught, the children will be ready to begin encoding words. When working with kindergartners, it is suggested that they not be expected to write the encoded words on paper. Writing small letters may be beyond their developmental level.[5] They will, however, use the large arm swings and gross kinesthetic-motor movements to form letters and reinforce recall of letter forms and sounds.

Young children often continue to need guidance in directionality. This refers to beginning at first sound of a word instead of the end (which is common with beginners and some older dyslexics). Also, it refers to the left to right letter placement in words. Therefore, the procedures for beginning encoding are slightly different from those used when working with older children.

The letters that have been practiced in handwriting, visual cards, and auditory cards will be used in this lesson. The keyword cards should be visible so that the children may refer to them if needed.

Alphabet cards should be placed in the correct order on the card chart. A piece of colored paper should be placed at the top of the chart to provide a background for building words. (The vowels are on salmon colored cards; consonants are on white cards.)

Teacher: "Today, we are going to use these sounds we know (point to letter cards on card chart) to spell or build some words. We will build our words on this colored paper. Before we begin to build words, let's practice our sounds."

Auditory Card Drill: Use letters h, l, b, t, f, c, r, m, and a.

Teacher: "What says /l/ as in lamp?"
One child is selected to respond: "l - lamp - /l/"
The child forms the letter in the air with an arm swing as he says the letter name. The group repeats while forming the letter with an arm swing.

After letters have been reviewed, the children are ready to begin encoding or spelling words from an auditory stimulus.

Beginning Encoding Steps for Advanced Groups

Choose a child to come to the chart to build a word. It is wise to give the first turn to a child who has shown strength during earlier phonemic awareness lessons such as Recognizing Embedded Units of Sound in Words—Ending Phonemes on page 62. Whoever is chosen, you assume the responsibility of guiding the child through to success.

Teacher: "Thank you, ___, for helping me teach the group how to build words. You don't need to worry, because I will be your partner in teaching this. Everyone will be paying close attention so that they will be ready for their turn. We will all be very quiet to give you a chance to think. Your word is hat. Let's all say the word hat."

Child encoding word.

Child substituting letter card representing sound in a new word at chart during encoding lesson.

The group responds with pronouncing the word <u>hat</u>.

Teacher: "Now, I am going to ask you some questions which will help you build your word. What must you listen for? You should say: I must listen for the beginning sound."

Child: "I must listen for the beginning sound."

Teacher: "What is the beginning sound? Say your word again and tell me what is the first sound that you heard and felt your mouth making?"

Child: "/h/"

Teacher: "What letter makes that sound? Please name the letter while you form it in the air."

Child: "<u>h</u>" while forming the letter with an arm swing in the air.

(You may need to help the child by saying the word and overemphasizing the beginning sound. Sometimes it is helpful to have the child start saying the word. Then signal the child to stop as he finishes the first sound. At other times, it is helpful to call attention to the movement of the lips, tongue, or teeth.)

Teacher: "Very good! Now, you may find the letter and say its name while you put it on our word holder (colored paper)."

Teacher: "Say your word again. This time, hear and feel the sound that opens your throat." (Teacher should place her hand on her throat to establish this as a hand signal.)

Child: "<u>hat</u> - /a/."

Teacher: "What letter makes that sound?"

Child: "<u>a</u>." The child forms the letter in the air with an arm swing as he says the letter name. (Forming the letter in the air assists the young child in recalling the letter and recognizing the letter.)

Then, the child places the vowel letter card next to the beginning card. The child should say the name of the letter as he places the card, <u>a</u>.

Teacher: "Say your word again. Now, hear and feel the last sound in your word."

Child: "<u>hat</u>, /t/."

Teacher: "What letter makes that sound? Name the letter while you form it in the air."

Child: "<u>t</u>." The child forms the letter in the air with an arm swing as he says the letter name.

Teacher: "Now, please say the name of your word and then put all of the letters together to spell the word <u>hat</u>."

While the group watches, the child names the letters while forming them in the air with a full arm swing: "<u>hat</u>, <u>h-a-t</u>."

Teacher: "Great! You have spelled our first word. Let's all say our word and spell it as we form it in the air."

Lead the group as they name the word and form the letters in the air with large arm swings: "<u>hat</u>, <u>h-a-t</u>."

The children should learn to overlap the alphabet cards so that the letters appear as a complete word rather than individual letters strung across the chart holder or board.

Examples of phonetic words and nonsense words that may be used in the beginning:

hat	tab	bat	lat	hal	mal	rat	lab
hab	tal	bab	lal	mat	ham	mam	at
fat	fab	fam	ram	rab	ral	mab	maf

It isn't necessary to spend a great deal of time finding phonetic words. A reference book of word lists has been prepared by Slingerland and Murray (1987).

Shortening the Encoding Procedure

During the first few experiences of encoding words with the alphabet cards, guide the children using the preceding script. As soon as the children can remember the steps, <u>limit your verbalization</u>. However, always be ready to intervene and ask the appropriate guiding question from the above script, which will lead the child to success. The child should not be allowed to fail at this task. It is your responsibility to be sure the child has been prepared adequately by knowing the individual letter sounds, and has been given an appropriate word for his individual performance level.

Beginners should work with consonant - vowel - consonant (c - v- c) words. It is easier for beginners to hear the sounds that are added after the vowel. When proceeding to longer words, after considerable practice with the smaller words, the consonants should be added following this pattern:

consonant - vowel - consonant (c - v - c)	(hat)
consonant - vowel - consonant - consonant (c - v - c - c)	(camp)
consonant - consonant - vowel - consonant (c - c - v - c)	(flag)
consonant consonant vowel consonant consonant (c-c-v-c-c)	(stamp)

Shortened Pattern for Encoding

Teacher: Name a word.

Child: Repeats the word, gives the beginning sound, names the letter that makes that sound while forming that letter in the air, and places the card while renaming the letter.

Child: Repeats the word, gives the vowel sound, names the letter that makes that sound while forming the letter in the air, and places the card while again naming the letter.

Child: Repeats the word, gives the last sound, names the letter that makes that sound while forming the letter in the air, and places the card while again naming the letter.

Child: Repeats the word and names the letters while forming them in the air.

When the word is completed, you and the child lead the group in saying the name of the word and spelling the word aloud while forming the letters in the air.

Helpful Hand Signals

Instead of the teacher "talking too much" (an occupational hazard), some hand signals are helpful when the child forgets the sequence. Holding the thumb and forefinger about two inches apart and moving them from left to right is an effective hand signal for the child to say the word. Touching your ear with your forefinger signals to give the sound. You may touch your throat as a hand signal to listen for the vowel sound.

Introducing a New Vowel

Slingerland recommends that only the short vowel a be used until the children have demonstrated a good understanding of the encoding skill. While considerable time is taken using this one vowel, waiting until the children are automatic in the encoding steps will ensure their learning and make the steps that follow much easier. Once this is automatic, new vowels can be introduced and used in a more rapid succession.

The second vowel to be introduced is the short i. This is because the discrimination between the sounds of short a and short i is so clear.

Only the short i sound should be used during the first several days after it has been introduced. After that, the two vowels, a and i, may be used interchangeably.

Vowel Discrimination

After the second vowel has been introduced, a new step will be added to the lesson. Following the Auditory Card Drill, (taught previously in Association from Auditory Stimulus—Auditory Cards and described again in Auditory Card Drill), a few minutes should be spent on vowel discrimination. In this procedure, you will work with only the two vowel cards.

Teacher: "Today, we are going to listen for the different vowel sounds in words. I will say a word. If it is your turn, you will repeat the word, listen and think about the vowel sound—the sound that opens your throat—and give me that sound. Then you will tell me the name of the letter."

Teacher: "trim."
Child: "trim - /i/ (short sound of i) - i" (while forming letter in air)
Teacher: "slim."
Child: "slim - /i/ (short sound of i) - i" (while forming letter in air)
Teacher: "ham."
Child: "ham - /a/ (short sound of a) - a" (while forming letter in air)

Following are more words to use during vowel discrimination procedures. (Note: this list is different from an encoding list. Children may not have been introduced to all of the sounds of the word, but they need only listen and focus on the vowel sound. In contrast, in an encoding list, the children must be familiar with all sounds (phonemes and graphemes.)

chap	slid	sprat	clasp	bib	brin	grin	crab	blast
ship	lamp	rift	gag	drag	limp	will	bad	stick
drill	track	trip	flash	flip	gasp	lift	crack	trash
zip	wilt	trill	wham	damp	wax	yap	pass	staff
hint	lid	ramp	lash	grass	limp	flat	rib	bid

As new vowels are added, they will be put in the vowel discrimination pack and put into encoding practice. The next short vowel will be u, followed by o. The short e sound is very difficult to discriminate and is held until later in the first grade to allow for further maturation. In the meantime, the first grade teacher will begin adding the long vowel sounds. Further information regarding sequencing, other areas of the language curriculum, and teaching procedures may be found in Beth H. Slingerland's *A Guide for Primary Teachers* (1971), and Carol Murray's *Scope and Sequence for Literacy Instruction* (2002).

Substituting Sounds in Encoded Words

The children should be very comfortable with the encoding process before the substitution step is introduced. If this has been accomplished, the substitution will be an easy step. Prior to beginning, discuss the meaning of the word "substitute."

Have a child encode the word hat on the card chart using the previously presented steps. When the word is completed, and the entire word has been seen and spelled aloud while forming the letters in the air, the new substitution step will be introduced.

Teacher: "Say the word hat, then say the word bat."
Child pronounces each word.

Teacher: "If that says hat (teacher points toward word), how could you make it say bat? Feel the difference in the way your lips move and the sound that you make. What part of the word hat will you need to change to make it say bat? The beginning, the middle, or the end?"
Child: "I need to change the beginning letter."
Teacher: "How will you change it?"
Child: "I will change the h to a b." (or something similar)
Teacher: "Very good! Now, a good way to say that is to say I will substitute the b (at this point pick up the alphabet card b) for the h (placing the b on top of the h)."

The child repeats: "I will substitute the <u>b</u> for the <u>h</u>, and places the <u>b</u> on top of the <u>h</u>."

Teacher: "Now, say the name of the new word and then spell your new word."

Child: "<u>bat</u> - <u>b-a-t</u>" while forming letters with full arm swing.

When completed, the group names and spells the new word aloud while forming the letters in the air.

Older children often remove the letter they are replacing; however, this can become cumbersome for the kindergarten child.

Shortening the Substitution Process

After the children understand the steps, the substitution procedure can be shortened.

Child encodes given word using previously learned steps.

Child leads group in spelling word aloud while forming the letters in air.

Teacher: "If that says <u>hat</u>, how could you make it say <u>ham</u>?"

Child pronounces both words, listening for the difference in the sounds.

Child: "I need to change the ending sound to /m/."

Child: "I will substitute <u>m</u> for the <u>t</u>." (Changing alphabet cards as he speaks).

When completed, the group spells the new word aloud while forming the letters in the air.

Some words to use in practicing this step:

1	2	3	4	5
tam	bat	hit	map	pan
ram	bag	bit	lap	ran
Sam	lag	sit	gap	ban
sat	lab	sat	gas	bin
sag	lat	Sam	gat	fin
sad	hat	mam	mat	fit

VISUAL APPROACH—BEGINNING DECODING FOR THE VERY ADVANCED GROUP

When the children have become automatic in encoding words, (i.e. they can encode words without teacher coaching), they are ready to begin decoding or "figuring out" printed words. <u>If they are truly automatic in their encoding skills, this will be easy to teach. If they are not automatic, that is, they really don't have the phonemic skills, decoding will be difficult.</u> In that case, more work should be done with encoding. Decoding is usually introduced about the time you teach the second vowel—the short sound of <u>i</u>.

Teacher: "You are doing so well in building words that we are ready to learn something new. First, we will do our Visual Card Drill."

(By this time, you should not have to tell the children what to do. The steps should be automatic.)

Visual Cards

This drill is done on a daily basis. It is just the opposite of the Auditory Card Drill.

Expose a card. An individual child should:
- Name the letter while forming it in the air.
- Name the keyword.
- Give the sound.

If the individual child was correct, the group repeats "h - house - /h/" while forming the letter in the air with a full arm swing.

Beginning decoding or sounding out the unknown word.

Teacher doing alphabet cards with child.

Beginning Decoding (Unlocking)

It is suggested that you refer to pages 153-173 in Slingerland's *A Guide for Primary Teachers* (1971).

Make the word <u>lab</u> in the alphabet chart. (After this first word, the letters can be printed on the board. This word was chosen because the letter <u>l</u> has an extended sound which makes beginning decoding easier.)

Teacher: "Today, I am making a word on the chart. This word begins with the same sound as the first letter in the word _____. (Child's name), tell me about the first letter."

The individual child should tell about the letter while forming it in the air: "l - lamp - /l/." (Children in first grade and above are able to discontinue giving the keyword during this activity. Kindergartners may still need the support.)

Teacher: "The next letter is the vowel whose sound will open your throat. Tell about the vowel."
Child: "<u>a</u> - apple - /a/."
Teacher: "Good! Now start making the sound of <u>l</u>, and while you are saying /l/, think of the way your throat opens to make the vowel sound, and put them together" (*Ibid*, p. 161).
Child: /l——a/ (short sound of <u>a</u>), /la/. As the child says: "/la/," you should move her hand or fingers from the beginning consonant through the vowel. It may be necessary to do this several times. You may also silently make the sounds so that the child can see your lip movement.
Teacher: "Work out the last letter so that you can finish your word."
Child: <u>b</u> - ball - /b/ while forming letter in the air
Teacher: Now, say /la/ again. Keep making the sound, and this time, add the last sound. (Again, move your hand under the letters as the child blends the sounds together to form a word.)
Child: /lab/
Teacher: "Excellent work! Let's all say her word with her." (or other reinforcing comment)
Group says word.

Some phonetic words to use in decoding practice include:

lat	lass	lad	man	mad	mass	nap	nan	van	ban
bad	bat	fat	jab	tan	lid	dim	rib	bid	mitt
sit	sift	lift	rift	list	last	fit	fist	kid	lap
ham	damp	lamp	ramp	gas	fast	back	camp	sash	tack
can	cab	tat	rat	tan					

Many more words can be found in the Word List Books (Slingerland and Murray 1987).
Children in first grade and above will be able to eliminate many of the supportive steps that kindergarten children need.

Visual Approach—Identifying the Vowel First in Decoding

After children become secure in hearing the first sound and beginning the word at the beginning rather than at the end (which is very common in kindergarten), change the procedure and ask the child to:
- find and underline the vowel while saying its name.
- give the vowel sound.
- begin at the beginning of the word, make the first sound, and keep making it while your throat opens up to make that vowel sound.
- finish the word.
- pronounce the word for the group.
The group repeats the word.

ACTIVITIES TO ASSIST CHILDREN IN ORAL EXPRESSION

Putting words together in meaningful sentences

This activity can be presented in a structured situation, but is especially effective in those "teachable moments" when a child has difficulty expressing his thoughts orally. A good example is during "sharing." Often, young children who are eager to share come before the group and then "freeze," standing silently in front of the waiting group. They usually know what they want to "share," but have difficulty in both organizing their thoughts and retrieving the words to express these thoughts. At this point, you may give gentle guidance, asking the child, "What do you want to talk about?" Child responds. Teacher: "What can you tell us about it? Begin with the words, "We went (or another appropriate beginning depending on the subject)."

A sample situation with teacher guidance might be as follows. The child has a picture of a puppy. It becomes obvious that the child is having difficulty in beginning to talk about the picture.

Teacher: "First, tell us what (or who) you want to tell us about."
Child: "My puppy."
Teacher: "Now, tell us something about your puppy."
If the child still has difficulty starting, you might ask, "What is this in your picture?"
Child: "Puppy."
Teacher: "Whose puppy is this?"
Child: "Mine."
Teacher: "Let's put those words together in a sentence. Begin with This is and then, tell us what it is."
Child: "This is my puppy."

Teacher: "Can you tell us what your puppy likes to do? First, tell us what you are talking about. My puppy and then tell us what your puppy likes to do."

Child: "My puppy likes to play."
Teacher: "What does your puppy like to play?"
Child: "My puppy plays with a ball."
Teacher: "What else can you tell us about your puppy?"
Child: "He is black and white."
Teacher: "Excellent! Now, can you put that all together and tell us about your puppy?" After working out sentences, give the child an opportunity to practice using the sentences. Of course, as time goes by, you can help the child elaborate on the phrases with questions such as, "What color is your puppy?" "How big is your puppy?" "Where did you get your puppy?" "What does your puppy eat?"

Watch the child closely in order to know when to give guidance and when to be quiet and let the child talk. Usually, once children get started, they are able to continue talking about their puppies or other chosen subjects. (Remember that teachers tend to talk too much; at the same time, the child should not be left in a failing situation.)

Children should always be encouraged to speak in complete sentences. Take time to help the children learn this important skill.

The strategy that should be emphasized is:

"What do you want to talk about?" Give time for response.
"What can you tell us about it?" Give time for response.
"Now, can you put that all together?" Give time for response.
Later, this can be shortened to:
"Start with telling us what you want to talk about, and then tell us about it."

Question of the Day: Slingerland Simultaneous Multisensory Approach to Language Arts

This strategy is used throughout the Slingerland Approach, with appropriate levels of questions and expectations according to students' age and abilities. It is a very effective way to help children learn to organize their ideas and speak in complete sentences. Hint: Using a portable microphone during this activity is a great motivator. Inexpensive ones may now be found in many toy stores as well as in the traditional music stores.

Ask the "Question of the Day," beginning at a simple level and proceeding to a more complex level as the children progress. Initially, ask the entire group, giving them time to think.

Then ask for five or so volunteers, or call on particular children. All five children come to the front of the group at the same time and stand in a straight line. (Having other children with them provides emotional support for the speaker. Helping them learn to stand in a straight line helps to prevent confusion and fidgeting.)

Repeat the question and then model the way to answer that question in a complete sentence.

The child answers the question in a complete sentence following the model that has been given. Stand by to give guidance and support. When the child is through speaking, he or she goes to the end of the line to provide support for the other speakers.

The procedure is repeated with the next child.

Example:

Day 1:

Teacher: "Our question today is What is your name and where do you live? I would like you to answer by saying, My name is ____. I live on ____ Street. I'll take the turn first. My name is Mrs. Brown. I live on Elm Street." Children take turns answering the question following the model.

Day 2:

Teacher: "What is your name? What is your favorite game? When you answer you should say, My name is ____ . My favorite game is ____ ." (It often helps for you to move your hand in an arch to show the group of words that should be phrased together.)

Help children learn to introduce themselves before answering the question by saying their names in a complete sentence. At a later date, the questions may be developed into more complex questions by asking, "What is your favorite game, and with whom do you like to play this game?" or "Why is this your favorite game?" "Who plays this game with you?" Other questions can include "what," "when," "where," "who," and "how." During this teaching activity, an oral model should always be provided.

In future years, you may write a Question of the Day on the board for the students to copy and answer as they enter the classroom. They will find this to be an easy exercise if the Question of the Day has been done orally during the formative language years and the children realize that the written question contains the spelling and most of the words they will need to write complete sentence responses.

Sample Questions

What is your favorite color?

Where do you see your favorite color?

What is your favorite food?

What is your favorite drink?

If you could choose to take a trip to anywhere in the world, where would you go?

What is the nicest thing that anyone ever did for you?

What is the nicest thing that you ever did for anyone else?

What do you like to do on Saturday morning?

Can you tell us something that is round?

How many people are there in your family?

Do you have any brothers?

Do you have any sisters?

If you had three wishes, what would they be?

If you could be an animal, what would you choose to be?

Which kind of a day do you like the best, a sunny day or a rainy day?

What kind of games do you play on a rainy day?

Retrieving Information and Words to Fit Context

This oral language exercise is especially suitable for use with preschool children. I have used it with 3- and 4-year-old children as well as older children with language processing problems. As you use this technique to extract language, the child will receive practice in recalling events, sequencing these memories, and retrieving a correct word to fit the context of the sentence. As time goes by, this activity will lead to the children being able to retrieve the information sequentially and become independent in retelling events. As this development occurs, encourage the children to tell more of the story and decrease your role (talking).

Successful implementation depends on:
- Using the exercise in close proximity to the time of the experience.
- Keeping vocabulary expectations within limits of the child's demonstrated, repeated use.
- Your or parents' experience in holding an interactive conversation with children. Adults need to listen and observe children closely to recognize when they are able to respond independently and when to prompt them.
- Pacing is very important. Time should be allowed for children to think and respond, but not enough time for them to become frustrated. Obviously, this is different in every case. Watching children's eyes and body language helps determine the pacing.
- With practice, you can prompt in such a skillful way that the children feel the success. In other words, don't tell them the answer, but help them find it for themselves, through nodding, pointing, acting, or other cues.

Examples of Discussions

A Visit from Grandparents

This first example actually took place with a 38-month-old child. Her grandmother and "Papa" had arrived at Tori's house for dinner and play. Upon arrival, Tori led Grandmother into her bedroom to read a book. When Tori chose a blank book (supplied by her mother for Tori to use in drawing pictures), it was the ideal teachable moment. She liked the idea of telling the story about her grandparents' visit. The underlining indicates the words Tori said (see below). She filled in the underlined words verbally when her Grandmother paused and indicated it was Tori's turn. This can be indicated through the tone of voice, nodding at the child, and looking directly into her eyes when it is her turn to respond. This is an oral language exercise with no writing by the child.

Grandmother: "Tori and her mother called Grandma on the telephone. Tori's mother said: 'Please come over and eat dinner with us.' Then, Tori talked on the phone. She said: 'Please come to my house. Come to the door and ring the doorbell. Come to my house to play.' (Note: She said a number of other things on the phone, but the story should be kept brief to hold her interest.) Grandma said, 'We would enjoy coming to your house for dinner and to play.' Papa and Grandma drove to Tori's house in their car.

When they drove into the driveway, Boris, the <u>dog</u>, was glad to see them. He started barking and wagging his <u>tail</u>.

Papa patted Boris' head and said, 'No <u>barking</u>.' Grandma rang the <u>doorbell</u>. Tori and her mother opened the <u>door</u>.

Mother said, 'Come in.' Tori said, 'Come and <u>play</u>.' She took Grandma's hand and led her into Tori's <u>bedroom</u>. Tori said, 'Let's read <u>books</u>.' She got one of her books from the <u>bookcase</u>. Grandma said, 'First, let's make up a story about Grandma and Papa coming to visit <u>Tori</u>.'"

Recounting Morning Activities at Preschool or Kindergarten

This story was immediately following Activity Time in a Kindergarten class.

Teacher: "We have had a busy morning. When we first came into our classroom you put your things in your <u>cubby</u>. Then you hung up your <u>coats</u>. When we came to the rug, we said <u>good morning</u> to our friends and sang our <u>Good Morning song</u>. Bobbie led us in saluting the <u>flag</u>. Raul told us about today's <u>weather</u>. David told us about the <u>calendar</u>. We called the roll and found out that we were all here except for <u>Ben</u>. Suzy said that Ben is <u>sick</u>. We hope he feels <u>better soon</u>. Then we sang a <u>song</u> about <u>colors</u>. We did an experiment and mixed two bottles of colored water to make a new <u>color</u>. The colors we mixed were <u>blue</u> and <u>yellow</u>. Our new color was <u>green</u>.

During Activity time, we chose our work stations. Bonnie, Suzy, and Raul wanted to <u>paint</u>. George, Nikki, and Bill worked with the <u>construction tools</u>. Debbie and Mary choose the <u>Memory game</u>. David and Enrique built an airport with the <u>blocks</u>. Mary and Maria choose the <u>playhouse</u>. We were all good workers. When activity time was over, we cleaned up <u>quickly</u>. Then we came back to sit on the <u>rug</u>."

Developing Group Stories

This is an effective and an enjoyable way to develop oral expression prior to written expression. It is recommended that a few minutes be devoted to this activity on a daily basis. I have successfully used the technique with various groups including with preschool and kindergarten children with limited English skills.

The activity can begin with the teacher naming the subject, or eliciting the subject from the children. Some questions that are helpful in eliciting the story include <u>who, what, when, where, how, why, and action words such as "did what."</u> The sequence or structure of the story may vary.

A sample might go as follows:

Teacher: "Today, let's make up a story about a mouse." (Use hand in arch as you say the phrase "a mouse" showing the words that go together.) "Let's describe the mouse. Should it be a big mouse or a little mouse?"

Child responds. "It's a little mouse."

Teacher: "All right, our story will be about a little mouse." (Making arch as you say "a little mouse"). "What color is the mouse?"

Child responds: "Gray."

Teacher: "Can you put that all together to tell us what the story will be about?"

Child responds: "A little gray mouse."

Teacher: "Tell me one word that tells an action that the mouse did."

Child responds: "Ran."

Teacher: "Where did he run?"

Child responds: "Into the woods."

Teacher: "Good. Let's put that all together."

Teacher and Children: "A little gray mouse ran into the woods." (Use hand in arch to reinforce the three phrases concept.)

At times, the children may change the words slightly. This is all right as long as they follow the structure that has been set by you for this particular story.

First phrase tells "what or who."
Second phrase tells "did what."
Third phrase tells "where."

Teacher: "Why did he run into the woods?"
Child: "To get away from the cat."
Teacher: "Can we put all of that into a long sentence? First we will tell who." (Use your hand in an arch over each phrase as you help the children form a sentence.)
Teacher and children: "A little gray mouse."
Teacher: "Did what?"
Teacher and children: "Ran."
Teacher: "Where?"
Teacher and children: "Into the woods."
Teacher: "Why?"
Teacher and children: "To get away from the cat."
Teacher: "Who would like to say that whole sentence by themselves?"
Child (or probably several children) will respond. If not, guide them through the sentence by asking who, did what, where, why, etc.
Child: "A little gray mouse ran into the woods to get away from the cat." (Child may respond with smooth sentence, without pausing, which is just fine.)
Teacher: "What did the mouse find when he got into the woods?"
Child: "He found a squirrel."
Teacher: "What did the squirrel say to the mouse?"
Child: "Hello, Mr. Mouse. Why are you running?"
Teacher: "What do you think the mouse answered?"
Child: "I'm afraid of the cat, (the teacher may need to interject "said the") said the mouse."
Teacher: "This is going to be a very good story. Let's see if we can tell the part we just made up together."
Group repeats story. "When the mouse got into the woods, he found a squirrel. 'Hello, Mr. Mouse. Why are you running?' said the squirrel. 'I'm running because I am afraid of the cat,' said the mouse.
Teacher: "Then what do you think the squirrel said to the mouse?"
Child: "The squirrel said, 'I know where you can hide. (You may need to interject the word "where." Do not interrupt if the child is able to continue without the your guidance.) You can hide in that tree stump.'"
Teacher: "What do you think the mouse said then?"
Child: "Oh! Thank you, Mr. Squirrel. I will hide in the tree stump."
Teacher: "What do you think happened when the cat came into the woods?"
Child: "The cat looked and looked for the mouse, but he couldn't find him."
Another child: "Then the cat went home."
Teacher: "Let's see if we can tell the whole story."

A child (or possibly several) will volunteer. If not, lead children in retelling the story and then ask for a volunteer. <u>Don't be concerned about the child recalling the exact words of the story if he is able to recall the salient facts (little gray mouse; cat; into the woods; squirrel and tree stump) and the sequence of the story, and speaks in complete sentences.</u>

Compliment the children on their work and carefully print the story for the class storybook. The children may want to paint pictures to go with the story.

Obviously, the story may proceed in many ways. You should give guidance with helpful questions according to the children's level of development. Items discussed may include actions, descriptions, feelings, and as children mature, humor.

Providing for this activity frequently will prepare the children for the day that they can write their own independent story. When their handwriting and spelling skills develop sufficiently, the children will begin writing the stories spontaneously. I have found that the children's first independent stories were often quite long and involved (sometimes two pages) because of their oral language training experiences. Allowing the students to share their stories (oral/dictated or written) with their classmates, and providing them with enough TIME to compose stories encourages children to become expressive writers.

LITERATURE FOR ENJOYMENT AND COMPREHENSION

Literature Adds Melody and Richness

Literature adds melody and richness to language. It also assists in learning to interpret feelings. Children should be given many opportunities to engage actively in listening, discussion, and dramatization activities. A wealth of wonderful books is available. The books of many modern writers such as Dr. Seuss, Maurice Sendak, and Shel Silverstein have become classics, just as traditional nursery rhymes and fairy tales are.

Kindergarten children especially enjoy stories in which they can imagine themselves as participants. Stories that include children or have animals acting like children— riding bicycles or having a tea party—are popular. Rhyming, nonsense words, or stories with a definite rhythm or cadence are appealing. These assist in developing inner language that prepare children for successful reading. Books that compare, such as *What Good Luck! What Bad Luck!* or *Fortunately* by Remy Charlip expand the understanding of language. Your local library and bookstores are full of these literary treasures.

Often, stories, poetry, and rhymes should be enjoyed just for the pleasure of listening. At other times, involve the child in some additional activities to further expand her language experience. Care should be taken, however, not to let the "activities" spoil the experience of just listening to the beauty of the selection. Some activities discussed in this chapter will extend the listening comprehension experience and provide the basis for later reading comprehension. These activities are also used effectively to organize recall after watching a film or play or even in discussing a playground event.

Techniques for Presenting Books

Whether reading a book, showing pictures, or leading a discussion, it is important for teachers to maintain frequent eye contact with the children. The key to doing this is to be well prepared and familiar with the materials. As you read a story, it is helpful to turn the book toward the children. As you complete each page, the book or picture should be moved in a smooth sweep from one side to the other to allow all the children to see the pictures clearly. You can establish a smooth rate of movement by silently counting to 20 as you move the book. This allows children on all sides to see clearly without boredom. You should read the book with expression, being careful to observe good phrasing. Remember that the reader is modeling the way to read for comprehension and enjoyment. This is your opportunity to use that hidden dramatic ability. While reading a story, it is useful to run a finger below the words, thus helping children associate spoken words with written symbols.

Dramatic Play and Creative Dramatics

Children enjoy dramatic play, whether it be re-enacting a story they have heard or creative dramatics. Accessories such as paper bag masks and puppets or hats often help the timid child be transported into the activity. Children should not be expected to memorize scripts, but rather to recall sequences and use their own language to express characters' thoughts. In re-enacting the story, you may provide the narration of the story with children creating the dialogue. In stories containing repetitive sentences, the whole group may join in repeating these sentences such as, "Who's been sleeping in my bed?" from *The Three Bears*, or "Who's that tramping across my Bridge?" from *The Three Billy Goats Gruff*. After much experience in this activity, more mature children may feel comfortable in putting on their own plays—without your narration.

In creative dramatics, you may set the stage by reading a poem or describing a scene. Continue to use descriptive words, as children are encouraged to create in their own way. Some activities include imitating leaves falling from a tree or elephants tramping through the jungle (their walk heavy, swinging their trunks, etc.).

Using Literature to Develop Comprehension

Some activities to expand language skills and develop comprehension during storytime include the following.

Recalling Often-Repeated Words and Phrases

Children enjoy filling in the last word or phrase of familiar stories. Occasionally, when reading a familiar story, pause and let the children supply the next word(s) from memory. Encourage them to join in when reading often-repeated words or phrases. For instance ". . . you can't catch me, I'm the gingerbread man."

Recalling Details

After reading a segment, help children recall details through discussion. For instance, after reading the first line of Jack and Jill ask, "What was the name of the girl?" "What was the name of the other child?" At times, the discussion should include other details such as, "Where did they go?" "Why?" "When?" "What?" "How?" "How many?" "What color?"

Vary the length of recall segments. Sometimes have the children recall details after you have read a sentence. At other times, read a paragraph, a page, or even the complete story. If the story has been broken up for the purpose of recalling details or other pertinent information, it should be reread for the pleasure of hearing an entire story.

Caution: Don't ask too many questions about any one story. Preserve the joy of just listening while teaching children how to gain and recall information. Remember that older children also enjoy hearing a good story.

Recalling Sequences

Many children have difficulty organizing and sequencing. After reading, discuss the sequence of events in the selection. At first, you will need to be more active in guiding the discussion. Be careful to diminish the amount of guidance as the children become adept at this skill.

"What happened first?"
"What did he do next?"
"Raul ran to the corner store. What happened after he went inside the store?"
"What do you think will happen on the next page?" (prediction)

As children become more adept in sequencing, hold up a large, laminated number card. When the children begin to recall the sequence, show "1" and ask "Who can remember how the story began?" As children recall the events sequentially, the contributing children line up in front of the class in a left to right progression. (A "cardless" variation of this is to have the children line up in front of a chalk or white board. As the first contributor goes to the front, write a large "1" above his head.)

After four to six children representing the sequence of the story are standing in front of the class, ask them each to tell their part of the story. (One or two sentences are sufficient for each event or sequence.)

After the children at the front of the room review the story, ask if anyone in the class would like to retell all the parts of the story. The volunteering child should stand by the appropriate child as he recalls his portion of the story. When using number cards, the child holding the card should hold up his or her card as that part of the story is recalled. When using numbers on the board to indicate the sequence, the "sequence child" should point to the number above his head. Several children should be given turns in recalling the story sequence with the "sequence children" providing visual cues.

Give children three or four pictures that can be arranged in the proper sequence while retelling the story. (This is most successful as a small group activity.)

Give children paper folded in thirds or fourths. Ask them to draw a picture showing what happened at the beginning of the story, what happened next, and what happened at the end of the story. Ask children to retell the story to you (or an aide) and then to take the picture story home to use in retelling the story to parents, guardians, grandparents, siblings, and friends.

Always encourage the children to retell their stories using complete sentences.

Interpreting the Story—Relationships and Inferences
Help children interpret stories through guided discussions with prompts such as:

"What made you think that the man was tired?"
"What did mother mean when she said, 'take turns'?"
"What is a prince?"
"How did Bobby feel about _____?"
"How did you know how Bobby felt?"
"How could we tell that he was sad?"
"Was it a boy or a girl? What word let you know it was a girl? Very good! The story did say 'she'."
"In this story, what did the word steal mean? When the story said 'steal home base' did it mean Danny took the base home? How is this word different from the word steel as in the steel framework?"

Interpreting the Story—Recognizing the Main Idea
Following the story, lead discussions that help children focus on the main idea of stories. One way to do this is to consider a good name for a story.
Examples:
"Which do you think would be a good name or title for this story? The Rainy Day or Bob's Trip to the Zoo?"
"Who can tell us what the story Yertle the Turtle was about?" (Encourage a few sentence summaries. Gradually, work this down to the main idea or theme.)
"Can you think of another name for this story, a name that will let us know what the main idea of the story is?"
"How is this story like the story we read about____?"
"How is this story different from the story we read about____?"

Forming Opinions Based on the Story

Children should be given practice in forming opinions based upon stories. This is in preparation for later reading for information. Again, this is best done through guided discussion. Some examples of forming questions based on a story are:

"Do you think it was a good idea for Alex to run after the dog?"

"What else could he have done?"

"If you had been Alex in this story, what would you have done?"

"Which of the following sentences is true about this story?" (Teacher gives the children a few sentences that are true about the story.)

"Which sentence is not true about this story?" (Teacher gives the children a few sentences that are not true about the story.)

"Which building material would you have chosen to build a house? Why?"

CHAPTER 3

Activities to Develop Visual Processing and Recall

According to Rosner (1975), a first step in developing visual perception is to identify the salient points. The following activities direct children's attention to visual details. Having children describe their work forms some association with the language areas of the brain. However, this first group of activities should be considered to be at the object level. The required materials are available from school supply companies. They are often found in the math manipulative section of the catalogues.

Peg Boards + Pattern Task Cards
Pattern Blocks + Pattern Task Cards
Pentominos + Pattern Task Cards
GeoBoards + Pattern Task Cards
Stringing Beads + Pattern Task Cards
Tangrams + Tangram Pattern Task Cards
Puzzles

When first introduced, children should have the opportunity to work freely, without designated patterns. It will be interesting for you to note the differences in the ways children develop their own patterns.

After a time of free experimentation, introduce the commercially produced pattern cards. These begin at a simple level and progress to fairly complicated designs.

After introduction, these materials should be made available at an activity center in the classroom.

As you will observe, these manipulatives are very useful for developing arithmetic concepts.

ACTIVITIES TO DEVELOP VISUAL PERCEPTION AND ATTENTION AT THE LANGUAGE LEVEL

Naming from Memory—Objects in a Large Group

Box of Objects #1
Place several objects in a jumble on the table. After a period of close observation, call upon three or four children one by one to look away from the table and name as many of the objects as they can. Interest in this can be maintained only while two or three or four children attempt it. While the one child names the objects from memory, the others look at the table. Gradually increase the number of objects.

Naming from Memory—Entire Group of Objects

Choose from Box of Objects #1

Place in a basket a large number of familiar objects.

From these, select three and places them on the table behind a screen (e. g., a pencil, a spoon, and a dollhouse chair).

The screen is lifted and the children are told to look at the objects.

After a few seconds, the screen is replaced.

One child turns his back to the table and the screen is again lifted so that the other children can see while the chosen child names the three objects. He must name all. All but one is not satisfactory. If he is unable to name all three objects, he is allowed to choose a partner to help him finish naming the objects.

New objects are placed behind the screen and another child is chosen to name the objects.

The number of objects is increased from day to day until a large number can be recalled.

When the game is being introduced, disregard sequence. However, take note of those with or without a feeling of left to right progression.

At a later time, the concept of sequence will be added.

Group Naming

Have a small group of children stand in a line before the class or group.

Select a child to close his eyes and name all these standing children. Before this game can be played, children should have had ample opportunity to learn and pronounce each other's names.

Noticing Change of Sequence in Groups of Objects

Choose from Box of Objects #1

Place two objects on a table. After a period for careful observation, these are laid aside. A child volunteers or is chosen. He or she goes to the table, picks up the objects, and places them in the same order as you placed them. Place other objects and another child reproduces the sequence (e.g., first child places a book and a pencil).

If the child is successful, reinforce the concept. "The book was first and a pencil was second."

Of course, if the pencil is placed first and the book second, the point has been missed. If, after the following guidance, the child has not corrected the order, the child may choose a partner to help him.

You might say: "Yes, there was a pencil and a book, but something is different. Do you know what is different?"

Second child places a dish and a spoon

Third child places a ball and a box

On successive days, or with successive children on the same day, the series can be lengthened to three, four, or even five or six objects that are to be arranged in the same sequence as that in which they were originally arranged by you.

After the first and second concept has been well established, you may introduce and substitute the words left and right for first and second.

This concept of sequence is of great value for future reading and spelling.

Naming Objects in Sequential Order from Memory

Choose from Box of Objects #1

Place several objects in a left to right sequence on a table. After a period of close observation, call upon three or four children, one by one, to look away from the table and name as many of the objects in sequence as they can. Interest in this can be maintained only while two or three or four children attempt it. While one child names the objects from memory, the others look at the table. Gradually increase the number of objects.

Group Naming in Sequential Order from Memory

Have a small group of children stand before the others in a line. A selected child closes his eyes and names, in the correct sequence, all these standing children.

Before this game can be played children should have had an opportunity to learn and pronounce each other's names.

Help the children learn to rehearse by:

Saying the names in sequence softly.

Then, by "saying them in your head." (This helps the children learn to use their inner auditory memory.)

Noticing Change of Sequence and Orientation in Group of Objects

Box of Objects

For this game, it is necessary to have articles that have obvious sidedness (e.g., a small pitcher with a handle, a spoon, a pair of scissors). Toy animals of metal or plastic, each two or three inches in length, lend themselves especially well to this purpose. There should be two identical sets of objects.

A child is given three objects (one set).

Arrange your duplicate set of three objects in a row. One object should turn toward the right, another toward the left. The group watches you as you place the objects.

After a brief period of observation for the children, cover the set with a screen. It is suggested that 15 to 20 seconds be allowed for observation. The length of the observation period may vary according to the abilities of the children. This is a learning procedure, not a test. If you observe that the selected child is subvocalizing the names of the objects in order to remember, adequate time should be allowed. Close observation of the child will allow you to know when you can cover the demonstration set.

The child with the duplicate set places his objects to correspond with his memory of the set that you have just placed.

The screen is then removed and the two sets are compared. Not only the sequence of objects but also the direction each is facing should to be considered. If the original exposure was

$$\rightarrow \qquad \rightarrow \qquad \leftarrow$$

and the child places his,

$$\rightarrow \qquad \rightarrow \qquad \rightarrow \quad \text{or} \quad \rightarrow \qquad \leftarrow \qquad \rightarrow$$

the results are not correct. Say, "Good try!" and help the child place the items correctly.

Then, this process is repeated with another child, using a different set of objects.

It sometimes requires much practice to get a child to realize that a pitcher with handle turned to the left or a dog headed to the right is not the same as a pitcher turned right or a dog headed to the left, even if the relation of the total objects to each other is correct.

In the future, children will realize that even though letters may be in the correct order in a word, if the letters are turned in a different direction, it will be unsatisfactory. Certain letters (e, g, b, d, p, and q) actually change their names and identity. But this fact is not introduced at present, merely the idea that the direction in which an object is turned is sometimes very important.

Memory Game (Concentration)

Use picture cards, made by using stickers on index cards, playing cards, or commercial Memory Game cards with matching pairs of pictures.

This is a small group activity for two or three children.

The object of this game is to remember where cards are placed and to collect as many pairs as possible. The child with the most pairs wins the game.

Cards should be placed face down in an orderly manner. Carefully placing the cards in a well-spaced square and showing the children to also use care in replacing the cards in their original sites, are important for aiding visual recall. The first child turns over one card, shows the card to the group, and then puts it face up in the exact place it had been. The same child then has the opportunity to turn over one other card in an attempt to match the first card. If the child has a matching pair of cards (i.e., two blue birds or two queens of hearts), he or she claims the pair and earns another chance to turn up two more cards. The child may continue turning over cards until he or she fails to get a pair. When a child fails to find a match, the cards are turned back over, face down, in their original position, and the next child has a turn.

As this game is being taught, the cards should be limited to three or four pairs (six to eight cards). When the children build skill, the number of pairs should be increased.

Cards should be laid out in an orderly, rectangle pattern.

Example:

```
X     X     X     X
X     X     X     X
X     X     X     X
X     X     X     X
```

Children should be taught to replace the card in the original position.

Colors

Today, the kindergarten child is often expected to recognize the color words. A helpful way to teach color words is to make a color collection.

Dedicate a week to each color. Mix food colors in attractive bottles. The child should attempt to predict what will happen when you mix red and yellow, etc. Print the color name on the label, which is placed in front of the color bottle.

Collect objects in the topic color. Print a card with the color word and place it with the color display.

Have the children wear the designated color with a printed color name label pinned on the pocket.

Make a color board containing examples of colors with color name labels attached. Perhaps this is a clown holding different colored balloons. Or weave a spider web out of yarn. Make large black spiders, each of which contains a large oval of color. The color name should be printed on the colored oval on the spider's back.

Play a matching game in which some of the children have a color word, and the other children hold pieces of colored construction paper in front of them. When the child with the color word approaches a child, he or she should say, "My color is _____. Do you have my color?" A color chart is conveniently placed in the room for reference by the children. Instead of just giving the name when a child asks for assistance in recognizing a color word, you should assist the child in finding the needed color word and discovering the color.

Labels and Signs

Using lower-case manuscript writing (printing), place labels on various items in the room. Items to be labeled might include playhouse, art table, paint easel, boys' restroom, girls' restroom, desk, chair, teacher's desk, door, puzzles, books, etc. At home, labels may be put on the bed, bookcase, dresser, closet, chair, and toy box. The purpose of these labels is to assist in "teaching before the fact." This promotes the association of the "squiggly marks" to words that have real meaning for the children. They should not be expected to read these labels, although many will learn to recognize the words through constant association.

Numerals and Number Names

Number names are also a part of language. Children need to develop a concrete understanding of numbers, recognizing the relationship between the figures and numbers of objects, etc. Most school curricula provide for this instruction.

Writing of numerals can be taught using the same tracing techniques that were used for teaching writing of letters (see p.74). Patterns should be left in a convenient place so that children can trace them with their fingers if they forget the formations.

As soon as they have an understanding of the basic Arabic numerals, the number words from one to ten can be introduced. It is suggested that these words be introduced on different days. Number words can be taught by using the Slingerland multisensory approach for teaching sight vocabulary (1996, pp. 176–179).

Write three or four words on a chart or chalkboard.

Say the name of the number word while holding a marker under the word. The children repeat the name of the number word while looking at the word. (This is a visual-auditory stimulus, with a kinesthetic response.)

Say the name of one of the words (at random).

An individual child repeats the word. Then, the child finds the word, holds a marker under the number, and pronounces the word. If the child is correct, the group repeats the word. If the child was in error, the group is to be very quiet while the child takes another look. In case of error, it is helpful for you to guide the

Multisensory Learning. The girl is receiving visual reinforcement by seeing the number pattern, auditory reinforcement as she hears herself say the name of the number aloud, and the kinesthetic feel in her arm, hand, and speech organs as she traces the large number pattern.

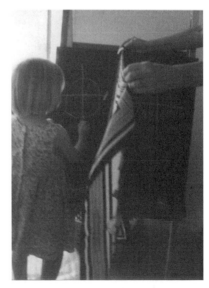

Multisensory Learning. Girl reproducing figure from memory.

child in starting at the top and working downward as they look for the correct word. When the correct word is found, the group repeats the word. (This is an auditory stimulus, with a visual-kinesthetic response.)

Ask other children questions such as:

"Find the number word that comes after three."

"Find the word that tells how many beats I am playing on the drum."

"Find the word that means the number which is equal to '1' plus '1'."

"Take the number of steps that this word says."

"Hop this many times." Clap four times. "Now, find the word that tells how many times you hopped."

The selected child finds the word, holds a marker under it, and says the number word.

The group repeats the word when the correct word is identified and pronounced. (This is an auditory concept stimulus with a visual-kinesthetic response.)

Select a child to read all of the words. The group repeats words after the child places the marker and correctly pronounces all of the words. Again, if there is an error, the group should be very quiet. (This is a visual stimulus with an auditory-kinesthetic response.)

Other activities to assist learning the names of the words may include the following.

Give the students patterns with the number or number word written in manuscript. Name that word. The children then trace the number or number word while saying the name of the number and then the names of letters in the word. At the conclusion, they name the word or number.

Make a list of four or five number words and four numerals in random order. Have a child draw lines to connect words with correct numerals and then draw the correct number of trees, suns, etc. to show understanding of number concept.

Have a list of four or five number words on a chart. Play a specific number of beats to correspond to one of the words on a rhythm instrument. Child identifies the number and finds the correct number word.

Variation:

Point to a word on a chart. Child then says the name and plays the correct number of beats on a rhythm instrument.

A few of the many available manipulatives.

CHAPTER 4

Activities to Develop Visual Recall with Kinesthetic/Motor Response*

DRAWING FROM MEMORY—GEOMETRIC DESIGNS

FOLDER 20 Geometric plane figures

Before this game is played, there must be lessons to learn the names of geometric plane figures such as square, rectangle, circle, and triangle. (Refer to Vocabulary on page 11.)

After the names are familiar, you may arrange the figures for the children to copy in the correct sequence.

Eye-hand coordination of individual children should be noted—those performing well, those with difficulty, and those refusing to perform.

Hold the passive hand of a child having difficulty, moving it to form a geometric figure. This is to strengthen visual association with the kinesthetic "feel" of the form. Tell the child, "Let's do this one together. Just relax and let me guide your hand."

After children have practiced drawing the figures, a game for recall can be played.

Arrange two figures for the children to observe for approximately 30 seconds. The figures are covered after the children's observation time.

Children draw from memory what they saw. When finished, your figures are exposed for comparison.

COPYING

FOLDER 21 Pictures of linear drawings

Make a simple, linear drawing, such as those in Folder 21, on the blackboard. The children copy it on paper with a crayon or large primary pencil. Each of these drawings has a one-sided form and is not correct if reversed, e.g.,

$$<$$

must not be reproduced

$$>$$

This copying should be done in the latter part of kindergarten and early first grade.

*In Association with Kinesthetic-Motor "Feel"

DRAWING PICTURES FROM MEMORY

FOLDER 21 Pictures of linear drawings

When a group of children has become proficient in copying from a seen object, the children can then be introduced to the concept of copying from a picture "seen in memory" (in their heads).

Simple drawings like those of the preceding game are drawn on the board, looked at carefully, and then erased or covered. Papers are distributed or other distractions provided. The children are told that during this interruption they are to remember the picture in their heads. After this break of a few seconds, they are told to draw the figure recently seen and erased.

Of course, the game permits no reversals. If this occurs, you should "talk the child" through the process of recalling in which direction the figure faced. If needed, allow the child to compare his picture with the original. Let him discover the difference without your stating that it is reversed.

The period between exposure and reproduction can gradually be lengthened, e. g., exposure before lunch, reproduction after lunch.

During this exercise, you will be able to detect those with accurate recall, those with accurate recall but poorly drawn forms, those with good forms but usually inadequately recalled, and those who are unable to perform. This information should be used in planning future instruction for individual children.

With some, this activity may suggest a need for more copying or tracing over your patterns to strengthen the kinesthetic "feel" in association with visual memory of form.

CHAPTER 5

Activities for Developing Tactile and Kinesthetic Recall

IDENTIFICATION OF AN OBJECT BY FEEL

One by one, place a pencil, a ball, a toothbrush, a comb, a toy spade, a doll's fork, etc. in a child's hand while he looks away. He names the object from the feeling.

It is better to have the child look out of the window or at the ceiling than to close his eyes, or still better, you can hold a large card before his face so the object cannot be seen. The other children can see but must not tell the child the name of the object.

After a turn, let the child choose another by naming the child, not by pointing to the one he chooses.

VISUAL-KINESTHETIC ASSOCIATION—BODILY MOVEMENTS

There are two sections to this exercise. The first involves imitation of movements. This should be mastered before the second section, involving sequential memory of the movements, is initiated. This should be a group activity.

In the first section, you and the children should be seated in a circle on the floor. As the exercise begins, say, "Watch carefully and then do what I do." Then, do something such as touching your left ear with your hand. All of the children in the group will then perform the same movement. If possible, this is done without talking (visual-kinesthetic association). For some children, it may be necessary to add the auditory stimulus by talking through the movements. The child sitting on your left should then say, "Watch carefully and do what I do." The group will then imitate that child's movement. Each child, in turn, will be given a turn in demonstrating a movement for the others to follow. As time goes on, the movements will become more complicated. For example, instead of touching the ear with the hand, the task may be to use the index finger, or a curled fist. Another child may choose to stand up and twirl three times, then sit down. Caution: As the exercise is taught, encourage the seated movements, rather than the ones requiring standing and moving. It is easier for children to focus the attention on the seated movement in which they can see the action clearly.

In the second part, after the children have become adept at imitating the movements, add the memory factor. The children should be reminded that if they "think or say what they are doing inside their head" it will help them remember what to do. The second child will first imitate the movement made by the first player, and then will add her own movement. The third child will imitate the first two children in sequential order before adding his own movement. This continues until a child forgets a movement. At this time, help the child by talking through each of the movements. Do not be discouraged if children forget after four or five movements. Experience has shown that this is about average for beginners. Continued practice will assist in retaining more information.

VISUAL-KINESTHETIC ASSOCIATION—ARM MOVEMENTS

FOLDER 20 Pictures of geometric shapes
FOLDER 21 Pictures of linear drawings

The geometric plane figures, together with some of the linear drawings, are placed in a row for all of the children to see.

Put a piece of chalk in one child's hand and hold a large card (approximately 9x12) before his face, as a screen. Move his hand to produce one of the figures on the blackboard or on a large piece of paper placed on the wall so all the children can watch. Then turn the child around so he cannot see what his hand has made, and stand in front of the drawing. The child, recognizing the shape made by his passive hand, selects from the row before him the one that matches his own. Not until then does he look at his own drawing.

Encourage and help the child to tell what his hand made.

At other times, move the child's passive hand to draw a simple form, e. g., an arrow, a chair, one of the geometric plane figures (the advantage in the latter being that the names of the figures are known).

In another game, the card is held before the child's face, as above, while his passive hand is moved to form some simple and known form. Without seeing what his hand made, he is asked to draw another form like it on another part of the board. Then they are compared.

All forms should be made at least a foot tall so the child's arm swing is from the shoulder.

KINESTHETIC DRAWING TO DICTATION

A figure designated by name is to be drawn with eyes averted or shielded.

"Draw a square."
"Draw a triangle."
"Draw a circle."

Encourage the child to make figures large enough to require an arm swing from the shoulder and not from the wrist.

KINESTHETIC DRAWING—PARALLEL LINES

Show the children how to draw a horizontal line on the board, approximately 12 to 14 inches.

Call upon a child to draw a horizontal line on the board.

Ask the child to make a dot two or three inches (show him) under the "first," "left" end of his line, and after placing his chalk on this dot, say, "Now, without looking, draw another line like the first one."

The child looks away and draws a second line from the dot, parallel to the first. He should try to make his new line just as long as the first. He then looks to compare the length of his two lines.

Older children may have pieces of paper to try this together, each child using a crayon or primary pencil.

Encourage an arm swing from the shoulder rather than from the wrist.

KINESTHETIC RECALL OF FIGURES

At a later time, after children have had experience with numbers and when letters are being introduced in first grade, Visual-Kinesthetic Association—Bodily Movements on page 107 and Kinesthetic Drawing to Dictation on this page can be used with number symbols and letters of the alphabet.

CHAPTER 6

Orientation Games

Many children need guidance in understanding words that tell position and size. Sequencing and memory are also important skills for children to develop. Encouraging children to "say the things inside your head" helps them learn to use their inner-auditory memory to remember items.

LEFT TO RIGHT PROGRESSION

Before the Visual or Kinesthetic Recall games can be played with maximum value, most children of kindergarten and first grade age need practice with directionality. The following are suggested.

- A row of five or six children stands up, and a designated child names each child in order from left to right. To many children, it does not occur to them that the "order" matters, if all are named.
- A row of familiar articles is arranged on a table, and various children are asked to name the articles in order.
- A row of pictures—a cat, a dog, a baby, a sled, etc.—are exposed to the group for naming.
- A row of numerals is exposed to the group for naming. Many children will name them hit or miss, 6, 5, 7, 3, 1, 2. A few will exactly reverse the series, 7, 6, 5, 4, 3, 2, and 1 due to confusion regarding the starting point.

Some form of this game should be played occasionally over a period of several months, until perfect orientation and naming is attained.

For children to have become thoroughly familiar and successful with such games will prove a great help in their beginning reading.

RELATIVE POSITION—BEFORE AND AFTER

These words are very perplexing to little children and older persons with confusion in progression and orientation.

Arrange a row of children, objects, or pictures. A train of cars, real or pictured, can be used. Touching a car, say, "The car comes after the engine." "The engine comes before the car."

A child touches one anywhere in the series and says, for example,

"The plate comes after the spoon."
"The knife comes before the spoon."
"The book comes after the box and before the vase."

In a variation of this game, give oral directions for placement.
Example: "Place the passenger car after the coal car and before the caboose."

RELATIVE POSITION—VERTICAL

Familiarity with the words "after" and "before" and practice in their use in both horizontal and vertical rows will be found of value in many situations. The concept, relative position, is an indispensable foundation for the acquisition of dictionary techniques.

When "after" and "before" have become familiar in horizontal positions, they should also be made applicable to vertical arrangements.

Numerals, objects, or pictures should be arranged vertically on a flannel board, magnetic board, tabletop, etc. A child will then respond to a question regarding one of the objects by describing its position.

Example
Teacher: "Where is the numeral 3?"
Child: "3 comes after 2 and before 4."
(Of course, when objects or pictures are used, the child names the object, not the numeral.)
In a variation of this game, give oral directions for placement. Example: "Place the picture of the ball <u>after</u> the picture of the house and <u>before</u> the swing."

RIGHT AND LEFT

In the Progression and Position games so far suggested, no reference has been made to the words "right" and "left." Many kindergarten children and older ones have not firmly established the significance of

Picture of children playing direction games such as Simon Says "touch your right toe."

these terms, even though hand dominance might already be firmly established. Many adults have great difficulty in following directions involving the use of these words. Some games like the following may be clarifying.

- In the beginning, the terms "right" and "left" are discussed with the children before the games are played. Place a large cut-out of a left hand on the left side of the room and a right hand on the right side (as the children face that position).
- Have all children stand up. Turn your back to the children and look over your shoulder as they practice lifting their right hand, tapping their left toe, touching their left ear, etc.
- When the children begin to seem secure about right and left, include the left and right directions while playing "Simon Says." In case anyone is unfamiliar with Simon Says, the direction must be preceded by the words "Simon says" in order to be a valid direction. If the children hear "Simon says . . . ", the children should follow the direction. If the words "Simon says" are omitted, the children should stay perfectly still. At first, just play the game without anyone being "put out." After children are secure with the game, anyone who performs the task when you didn't say "Simon says," or fails to perform on "Simon says," is out (sits down).

Examples:

"Simon says touch your right toe." (Children should touch right toe.)
"Clap your hands." (Children should remain still)
"Simon says: Hop on your left foot." (Children should perform task.)
"Raise your right hand." (Children should remain still.)

- One child is placed with his back to the group so all are facing in the same direction. He is told: "Turn your head to the left." "Put your right hand on your head." "Raise your left hand." "Lift your right foot." "Put your right hand on your left ear." Then he may choose another child. Eventually, individual children can give the directions.

USING TOUCH TO IDENTIFY THE LEFT OR RIGHT PART OF THE BODY

A child is seated, as in the preceding game, with his back to the group, but he covers his eyes. You, or later another child, touch him and he is to reply,

"You touched my left shoulder."
"You touched my right elbow."
"You touched my left knee."

It sometimes helps if a child is led to remember that his ring is on his left hand, or that his broken tooth is on his right side, etc. A piece of colored yarn may also be placed around the right wrist.

DUPLICATING SEQUENCE WITH COLORED BLOCKS OR BUTTONS

BOX 3 Colored blocks or buttons

This activity involves visual memory and left to right orientation. As the skill is taught, the auditory stimulus is employed as you "talk through" the procedure. Additionally, the child is receiving instruction and practice in using "inner-auditory" skills.

Place four blocks in a straight row, beginning at the left and working toward the right, while the child watches. As you place the blocks, say, "The first block is a red block." As you place the next block, say, "The second block is a yellow block." This continues as you place the four blocks. Then ask the child to place his blocks in the same way that you placed your blocks. In the beginning, you will probably need to help the child talk through the procedure.

The second step removes the spoken word, but encourages the child to use the "inner-auditory," or "Say or think the color name inside your head to help you remember." At this time, carefully place the blocks in the left to right sequence.

For example, when you place a red block, the child should think, "The first block is a red block." As you place the next block the child should think, "The second block is a yellow block." As the child become proficient at duplicating your color pattern, additional blocks can be added.

DUPLICATING SEQUENCE WITH COLORED BLOCKS OR BUTTONS FROM MEMORY

BOX 3 Colored blocks or buttons

When the child has become proficient in duplicating the left to right sequence with the colored blocks or buttons, add the element of memory. Again, remind the child to "Say or think the colors inside your head to help you remember which comes next."

Place three blocks, working from left to right, while the child watches. Nothing is said. After pausing approximately five seconds to let the child look at the sequence, hold a large card in front of your sequence of blocks and ask the child to make the block pattern just like yours. When the child finishes her pattern, remove the blocks and help the child talk through the sequence such as, "First we placed the green block, the second block was red, etc."

If the child "freezes" due to forgetting the blocks, coach him to say the color names to himself. If difficulty continues, say, "First we placed the . . . " (pause for the child to have time to think). If trouble still persists, move your card and say, "Take another look and say the colors to yourself." Remember that once you give the task, it is your responsibility to help the child complete it successfully. This is not a testing situation, but rather a teaching one. Keep it an enjoyable activity.

FOLLOWING RIGHT AND LEFT DIRECTIONS—STEPPING

Many children have difficulty following a series of directions. This can improve somewhat with practice. Children should be taught to repeat the directions. At first, the directions should be repeated aloud so that they can reinforce their memories. The next step is to have them repeat the directions "inside their heads" using their inner auditory memories. Begin with two or three directions, and gradually increase the number of directions, depending on the individual child's needs.

Prior to beginning this exercise, the group should have a good understanding of right and left. They must also have had success in following a sequence of two or three simple directions that do not depend on right and left orientation.

Examples:

"Put your hands on top of your head, take them down, and clap three times."

"Walk to the drinking fountain, have a drink of water, come back to the group, and sit down."

Examples of directions including right and left orientation are:

"Walk two steps straight ahead, turn left and take one step, then turn and walk three steps to the right."

"Stand in front of your chair, turn to your right and walk to the teacher's desk, touch the desk, turn around, and skip back to your seat."

The girl is recognizing the unseen shape by the kinesthetic feel as the teacher guides her hand.

"Turn around two times, walk three steps to the right, touch the floor, stand up, and hop three times on your right foot."

POINTING TO OBJECTS TO THE RIGHT OR LEFT

A child stands with his back to the group so that all see the same scene.

He is told to point to various objects, the locations of which are known (e. g., door, window, blackboard, sandbox), using his right hand for an object on his right, and his left hand to point to ones on the left. After he has understood this use of the proper hand for each object, he closes his eyes.

Directions for pointing are renewed.

It is not unusual for the entire field of vision to become reversed, so that he points to the vase of flowers on his right with his left hand and over to the left side.

RELATIVE POSITION—RIGHT AND LEFT, BEFORE AND AFTER

Ask a child to stand before the group with her back turned to them. Ask another child to stand on the <u>left</u> side of the first child, or the <u>right</u> side. Sometimes ask the child to stand <u>before</u> or <u>after</u> the first child.

After familiarity with the game, three children can stand with their backs to the others.

The middle child is asked to tell who is standing at his <u>right</u> side or <u>left</u> side. The outside children can be asked to tell where the middle child is in relation to them.

PLACING AND "READING" SHAPES IN LEFT TO RIGHT SEQUENCE

Each child has a large piece of construction paper and cutout shapes including a triangle, square, rectangle, and circle.

Review shapes, then ask the children to hold up the square, circle, rectangle or square, and triangle. This begins the first part of the game.

After a brief modeling, direct the children to place the cutouts on the construction paper in a given left to right sequence. They then "read" the sequence (left to right) "square, ____, ____, ___."

After you have led a group activity in placing shapes and "reading" several different sequences, ask the children to make up their own sequences.

Then give the children the opportunity to read their own sequence, being sure that their reading moves from left to right.

SEQUENCE GAME—PACKING FOR AFRICA

This is a game that helps the child practice remembering things in sequence. At the kindergarten level, the child does not have the use of alphabetical order, but needs to remember the items in sequence. The first player starts by saying, "I am going to Africa and I am going to take (names item)." Each player repeats the sentence, names the previously named items, and adds his own item to the list. This continues until someone misses an item. Then a new game is begun. When older children play this game, the element of alphabetizing should be added. The first player will name something beginning with the letter "a." The second player will repeat the sentence and name the previous item which began with "a," and then add an item beginning with "b." This continues with each person naming the previous items and adding his own item according to the next letter in the alphabet. Again, the game stops when someone misses an item and a new game is begun.

TOUCHING SEQUENCE GAME

This game is played silently, but involves the child practicing using "inner-auditory" messages. Children take turns silently, but plainly, touching one item in the room. The next player touches the first item and then chooses another item. This continues until someone forgets the sequence.

The children should be sitting in positions in which they all have clear views. As you prepare to play this game, remind the children about "saying the name of things inside your head" to help remember. Taking a few minutes to practice this technique helps the children become accustomed to use their "inner-auditory" skills.

Tell the children, "Today, we are going to practice using our memories. Watch closely; I am going to touch one item. I won't say its name and no one else should say it aloud. We will be very quiet, but, of course, we will say the name of the item inside our heads to help us remember it. Then I will choose someone else to come up and touch the item I touched, in the very same place. If they can remember and touch the same place, then they will get to choose another item to be touched. Remember, don't say anything aloud; just say it inside your head."

Touch a prominent item, such as a flower vase or the back of a certain chair. Signal the children not to say anything by putting your finger in front of your lips. Then sit back down and select a child to touch the item you touched. Everyone remains quiet. If the child is successful in touching the first item, say, "Now you choose another item. Everyone should watch closely, because now you are going to have two items to remember." The next child must remember to touch the first item (the one you touched), the second item, and then (if successful) the child touches a third item to be added to the game. This continues until someone forgets the items in sequence. (This often happens around five or six items.)

If the child fails to touch the exact item, the game ends and a new game is begun. Choose someone to touch a new "first" item.

Section II

Why Are These Exercises Helpful?

OVERVIEW OF NEURAL AND LANGUAGE DEVELOPMENT

Some information in this section has been adapted from the
Workshop on Early Brain and Child Development, from Science to Practice:
A Workshop on Creating Presentations for Physician Leaders presented by the
American Academy of Pediatrics Early Brain and Child Development Planning Group.

The author is grateful to Robert Perelman, M.D., Director,
Department of Education of the American Academy of Pediatrics,
and the American Academy of Pediatrics
for allowing the inclusion of their work
and to Marc A. Lerner, M.D., Clinical Professor of Pediatrics, University of California, Irvine,
for his encouragement, guidance, and critique in preparing this material.

CHAPTER 7

Early Neural Development

NEURAL DEVELOPMENT: NATURE VERSUS NURTURE?

All behavior and development, whether it is social, motor, cognitive, or emotional, involves the brain. Although there is much remaining to be learned about the brain, the explosion of technology in the last few years has allowed great advances in our understanding of this miraculous organ. It is now recognized that there is not a valid basis for the "nature versus nurture" argument. Brain development depends on experience and genetics working together in a bi-directional relationship (Nelson 1997; Healy 1990). Both play important roles in development, with the environment influencing natural development, even prior to birth. The time course of these developmental changes varies within individuals. The influences of stress, nutrition, and exposure to toxins such as alcohol, smoke, drugs, and chemical fumes have been demonstrated in numerous studies. More subtle influences, including language used in the environment, have also been shown to have effects in modifying development, even while babies are in utero.

Brain development begins before birth and continues throughout life (American Academy of Pediatrics 1999; Nelson 1999). The first three years of development after birth are most important because they provide the foundation for all future development. The brain has a great deal of plasticity, particularly at this early stage. It is capable of recovering from many insults or injuries. It is true that damaged brain cells cannot be repaired or replaced; however, research demonstrates that if brain damage is detected early, other cells may take over the functions of the damaged cells (Nelson 1999). When one pathway is blocked, another often takes up the task of the blocked pathway.

Although there is a general pattern of development, time variances occur within individuals. It is important that children receive stimulation targeted to their neurological maturation. For young children, this translates to language, language, language! Read to children. Talk to children. Listen and interact with children. Assist them in labeling and categorizing objects in their environment. Expose them to language. The importance of oral language was recently emphasized by the American Academy of Pediatrics (August 1999) in a policy statement discouraging the use of television with children under two years of age. Too often, television replaces a child's interaction with adults. Passively watching and hearing language on television or a computer is not the same as participating actively in oral communication.

A BRIEF INTRODUCTION TO NEURAL DEVELOPMENT FOR TEACHERS AND PARENTS

Children should be exposed to enriching experiences, but should not be forced to perform tasks for which they are not neurologically ready. There are physiological processes that cannot be rushed. One of these is myelination, or the gradual covering of the neural pathways with a fatty-like insulation. Myelination is necessary for neural connections to function effectively because it increases the speed of conducting information from one neuron to another (Nelson in press; American Academy of Pediatrics 1999).

At birth, the brain is quite disorganized with billions of neurons and glial cells. Glial cells function in a supportive, nurturing manner and are the source of myelin. The neural cells (neurons) are communication centers, receiving and sending information. These cells are responsible for our thoughts, movements, and senses. Each neuron is capable of communicating with thousands of other neurons. Synapses, the connections between neurons, are strengthened and become increasingly efficient and automatic as they are used. Extraneous neurons die as networks that are not stimulated disappear (Healy 1990). The surviving networks will be those that have been formed and strengthened through repeated use.

Synapses are the sites where neurons meet. It is here that the information is passed from cell to cell. Chemicals called neurotransmitters or neuromodulators facilitate the development of these synapses or neural connections between neurons. These same neurotransmitters act as chemical signals as information passes through a circuit of neurons. As this action is repeated, synapses are formed, modified, or strengthened. When neural pathways receive continued reinforcement through use, they become strengthened. When brain cells fail to receive appropriate stimulation, the neurons eventually stop "firing" or sending out messages. A lack of stimulation during the critical developmental periods may result in weak synapses that will be lost in "pruning" (loss of extraneous neural connections). Thus, experiences influence and actually change the basic "wiring" of the brain.

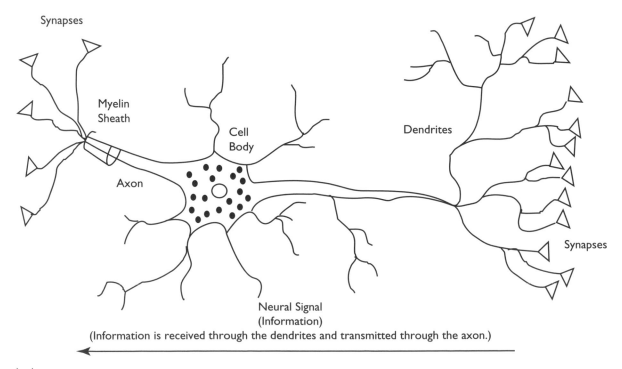

Developing neuron.

THE IMPORTANCE OF MYELINATION

The neural system, overall, is remarkably responsive to stimulation from the environment; however, the schedule of myelination appears to put some boundaries around "appropriate" learning at any specified age. Brain regions do not operate effectively or efficiently until they are myelinated. Prior to the completion of myelination, tasks are accomplished only through very tedious, labor-intensive, and energy-absorbing work.

The neural cells gradually develop an insulating coating of myelin, which facilitates rapid and clear transmission. Myelin develops slowly through childhood and adolescence. It is not completed until individuals are in their twenties, and for some, this process is not completed until a later age. Myelination gradually progresses from the lower to higher level neurological systems. This transition correlates with the ability to function mentally at an increasingly higher level. A case in point is the difficulty many children have in holding pencils and writing at an early age. Myelination of the neuromotor system develops gradually from "gross motor"—large, global movements—to the smaller muscles farther away from the core of the body (Healy 1990). Children's hands and fingers are often not ready for the writing tasks that are expected of them too early in many preschool and kindergarten environments. As a result, they may hold the pencil and form letters in an awkward manner. The tasks consume a much higher level of energy, with an awkward, difficult, and tiring performance. Avoidance behaviors may begin to surface. Continued incorrect performance results in the formation of a strong network of synaptic connections, making these maladaptive patterns automatic and difficult to change. Care should be taken not to rush children into writing too soon. Specific instruction on how to hold a pencil and form letters is essential to prevent maladaptive patterns from becoming automatic. This same care should be given to other tasks.

Care must also be taken in the way children are presented with stimulation. Young children take longer to process information than older children and adults. They have great difficulty when a stimulus is presented too fast, is unclear, or when they are bombarded by multiple stimuli simultaneously. Children become overwhelmed or tend to focus on the one aspect of the stimuli that fits their greatest personal interest, or need, which may not be what is intended to be learned. Multiple, simultaneous stimuli confuse children and usually defeat the purpose of stimulation.

Interestingly, developing skills early does not always guarantee continued success. The child who is a late walker may become the "star athlete," while the early walker may never develop skills at the "all-star" level. By the second grade level, it is usually difficult to identify the children who have been able to "word-call"[6] in a "stimulus-response"[7] type of activity at a preschool age.

THE DANGER OF FORCED LEARNING AT INAPPROPRIATE DEVELOPMENTAL STAGES

Educators and parents are cautioned to keep activities appropriate for an individual child's age and developmental level. There are potential hazards in trying to make children master academic skills prior to maturation (Healy 1990). A child may develop an aversion to a particular learning task. Forcing reading and written language tasks before readiness runs the risk of fear of failure, and may cause a borderline language disabled child to become truly disabled by compounding the original problem. This is not to say that books should be avoided. READ to your child. DISCUSS stories with your child. TALK to your child. LISTEN to your child. OBSERVE your child's activities when she is free to make her own choices. When the child is ready to begin reading, she will give you clear signals of her interest and ability in recognizing and recalling printed words. Motivation will not be a problem, as the developmentally ready child is highly motivated to read.

CHAPTER 8

Early Language Development with Suggestions for Stimulating Brain and Language Development

Usually, children who become fluent in language at an early age will have developed a better store of knowledge than will those with language delays. The environment further influences this natural difference. When children speak early, this ability is further influenced as they receive more responses from adults and others in their environments. Everyone joins in to encourage toddlers when they begin to repeat words. As a result, these early talkers receive more language stimulation than they would receive if they had delayed speech.

EARLY STAGES OF LANGUAGE DEVELOPMENT

During the first years of life, foundations for the understanding and use of language are laid. This is a necessary prerequisite to future learning through reading. Inner-language develops mainly through listening, talking, and playing. This is a critical time in the life of a child. More than 90% of brain development occurs during the first three years; however, development continues throughout life.

Experience plays a key role in the incredible development of the brain. The quality of the experience cannot be over-emphasized. Healthy brain connections depend on healthy human connections. Babies are born ready for human contact. They benefit from being surrounded by consistent, predictable experiences. The most critical factor is the attachment between parent and child. Early on, a baby needs to form a secure attachment to at least one caregiver. This early attachment affects children throughout life in that they learn faster, feel better, make friends easier, and generally do better. You can facilitate this attachment through touch, facial expression, voice tone, and your responsiveness to cues your baby gives to you. Caress, massage, and cuddle your baby often. Remember to be gentle when responding to cues given by your baby. Respond quickly when your baby cries. At this point, a baby needs help in structuring smooth regulated patterns and schedules. This will help any baby learn that the world is a safe, predictable, and loving place.

As children develop, they naturally use play, rhymes, and stories to develop language skills. They enjoy word games and spend much time "playing" with words. By providing specific opportunities and guidance, parents and teachers can enhance the way children play with language and greatly improve their learning and future.

Suggestions for Stimulating Brain and Language Development
(American Academy of Pediatrics 1999)

* Be consistent in the way you care for your baby.
* The most critical factor is attachment between the parent and child.
* Facilitate attachment through your facial expression, and your tone of voice.
* Touch, caress, massage, and cuddle your baby often.
* Be gentle and responsive to the cues given by your baby.
* Respond quickly when your baby cries.

PRENATAL LANGUAGE DEVELOPMENT

Language is developed naturally by a child's exposure to what he hears. Nature and nurture work together to foster this development. A newborn infant appears to be born with the necessary equipment and a ready expectancy for language. Then, the environment assumes responsibility. We now know that environment influences language development even prior to birth. While still within the womb, the fetus is able to hear sounds and recognize the mother's voice. There are also indications of early language neural lateralization. Electroencephalogram studies have indicated that different sides of the neonatal brain responds more to human voices (vowels) than to inanimate sounds (Molfese, Freeman, and Palermo 1975).

Some degree of familiarization with individual speech sounds also occurs prenatally. An interesting study on segmented learning prior to birth was done by Leucanet et al. (1989). Stethoscopes with loud-speakers were placed on expectant women's abdomens during their last trimester (between 35 and 38 weeks). Stimulus words included the spoken "bibi" and/or "baba." Significant cardiac deceleration occurred during the first few seconds of word stimulation. This deceleration reoccurred when the stimulus word was changed. These studies demonstrated that while still in utero, the infants were able to distinguish the differences made by changing the vowel sounds. "Phonological awareness" had begun.

AGES 1 TO 3 MONTHS

Newborns respond preferentially to stimuli that are familiar. During the first hour of post-natal life, newborns orient to both faces and voices. In the first day of life, a baby shows a definite preference for its mother's voice. A number of studies have demonstrated differences in babies non-nutritive sucking rates when exposed to different voices, including those of their mothers, other females, fathers, other males, and silence (in decreasing order of preference) (DeCasper and Fifer 1980; Moon and Fifer 1989; Moon and Fifer 1988). Another study indicated that at birth, babies could distinguish different languages. They could distinguish between sentences spoken in Japanese and Dutch. Ramus et al. (2000) concluded that rather than just isolating syllables, the babies processed enough information in a complete string of speech units to discriminate between the two languages. Again, non-nutritive sucking was used in measuring this task. Babies have also demonstrated their ability to imitate facial movements at less than one hour after birth. Although they appear to be born with some of these abilities, they are already responding to and being shaped by their environment (Meltzoff 1986).

During these first three months, babies begin to develop control of their bodies. At approximately two months, babies are able to lift their heads. Their interest in what they see and hear increases. Interaction with those in their environment increases and they begin to smile.

Soon, babies begin to gurgle and coo as they respond to people in their environment. At an early stage, babies learn to recognize and interpret the emotion and tones in their parents' voices or those of others in their environment. Mothers can readily attest to the reactions of babies when parents are upset and tired. They express their needs by crying. Mothers become aware of the varied cries their babies use to express their different needs.

Faces hold a special interest for babies; however, they soon lose interest if a face is expressionless. Observations indicate that disconnection occurs when a caregiver's face is blank. At that time, the baby appears to become disorganized with arms and legs flailing aimlessly.

Suggestions for Stimulating Brain and Language Development (American Academy of Pediatrics 1999)
Ages 1 to 3 Months

- Provide lots of warm, physical contact to give children a sense of security and well being.
- Caress, massage, and cuddle your baby.
- Use animation as you let baby examine your face.
- Play peek-a-boo.
- Show and discuss children's picture books and family photos, especially those including your baby.
- Show your baby his face in a mirror.
- Provide a special child-safe mirror in baby's crib or play area.
- Provide colorful play objects in different shapes, sizes, and textures.
- Actively respond to baby's gestures, faces, and sounds.
- Read aloud while holding your baby.
- Remember, the more words a child hears, the faster she learns.
- Talk and sing to your baby while dressing, feeding, bathing, playing, and walking.
- Talk, talk, talk! Tell your baby what you are looking at and describe your activities.

(Adapted from American Academy of Pediatrics 1999)

Twelve-week-old baby responds with smiles, gurgles, and coos.

AGES 4 TO 7 MONTHS

This is an exciting developmental time in the lives of babies and their caregivers. During this period, babies begin grasping items and rolling over. They are able to lift their heads and shoulders and support themselves on their wrists. By the sixth month, they reach for things with both hands and are sitting up.

At this age, babies are becoming more aware of their surroundings. The attachment between the baby and his caregivers becomes very strong. Some babies may be uncomfortable around strangers. Parents must watch for cues as to when their baby is ready to meet new people.

For most babies, self-initiated sound play and babbling begins at approximately four months as the babies prepare themselves for oral language. Locke (1993) suggests "that infants are aware of auditory-motor equivalence's well before the babbling stage," (p. 200). This suggests that there is a pre-adapted "expectant" neural capability for speech, which is activated by no more than token exposure to stimulation. They want to communicate and are becoming better able to make known their emotions and desires. Around five months, they begin articulating several syllable units. The onset of rhythmic vocal activity coincides with the onset of rhythmic movement of hands, at about six or seven months. At around six months, their babbling begins to reflect the specific language in their environment.

Suggestions for Stimulating Brain and Language Development
(American Academy of Pediatrics 1999)
Ages 4 to 7 Months

- Continue talking to your baby, face to face.
- Mimic the baby's sounds.
- Read books aloud. Tap or point to pictures and words.
- Enjoy music with your baby through dancing, listening, and singing.
- Continually watch baby for cues.
- Continue earlier activities.

Auditory discriminatory abilities begin to emerge during the first 12 months, with some infants displaying this ability during their first six months (Eilers and Minifie 1975). Some infants experience numerous ear infections during early childhood. Some researchers have suggested that these may interfere with the development of auditory skills, and sometimes these temporary hearing problems may complicate a pre-existing difficulty with phonemic awareness and other language-learning weaknesses. Although numerous ear infections have not been shown to be a cause of specific language learning disabilities (developmental dyslexia), the absence of stimulation received from hearing language during this critical developmental period may interfere with the strengthening of key neural pathways.

Environment and culture deserve credit for stabilizing the sounds that will become part of an individual's speech. Babies babble as they experiment with sounds. Soon, their repertoire of sounds is very large with many more sounds than are found in any language. The kind and number of sounds in different languages varies. The language the child hears in his or her environment reinforces the preservation of babbled sounds and syllables. Sounds not heard or reinforced in the environment will disappear or be "pruned" as the neural system becomes organized and prepared for oral language. When sounds are appropriate for a particular language in a child's environment, they are not pruned out of the babbling repertoire.

A good example of this can be seen in comparing the sounds /m/ and /r/ in American English. The sound /m/ is very common in babbling and is the most popular phoneme (language sound) in the world. It can be found in 97% of all languages. The /r/ in American English is the least frequent phoneme in the world. It can be found in fewer than 5% of languages. Thus, children living in cultures speaking the other

95% of the world's languages will have the /r/ pruned from their repertoire (Locke 1993). The best indication that children are acquiring phonology is that they are gradually relinquishing their extra non-native language sounds or phonemes.

Big sister reads book to baby.

Baby interested in book being read by grandmother.

AGES 8 TO 12 MONTHS

Often during this period, children become more mobile. They begin to stand and learn to walk around furniture while holding on for support. Babies in this age range begin to learn how to feed themselves, beginning with "finger foods." By the time they are around 12 months old, they begin to understand that a toy continues to exist in the last place that they saw it.

At this time, babies are becoming more expressive. During the early months of their lives, babies have been busy observing and listening to the sights and sounds in their environments. Now, they will begin attaching the meaning to the words that they hear. During this critical developmental period, the caregivers should immediately name an object when their child looks at it. This strengthens the association of a naming word with an object.

Imitation of sounds begins at around nine months. Babies use their voices intentionally in communicating with their mothers at around the age of 11 months, although this may not be necessarily with words. They also use gestures in meaningful ways. As development continues, children associate the auditory modality and kinesthetic (memory of movements) modality with their motor skills to develop speech. This demonstrates an awareness of the relationship between heard auditory patterns and seen oral-motor configurations (Dodd 1979; Kuhl and Meltzoff 1982). Some children may speak their first recognizable words around the time of their first birthday, although this time varies.

**Suggestions for Stimulating Brain and
Language Development
(American Academy of Pediatrics 1999)
Ages 8 to 12 Months**

- Stimulate hand-eye coordination and fine motor coordination by providing blocks and soft toys during playtime.
- Stimulate memory skills by playing games such as peek-a-boo and patty-cake.
- Be sure toys are age-appropriate and child safe. Double-check for small parts.
- Teach your baby to wave "bye-bye" and to indicate "yes" and "no" by shaking her head.
- Continue to read aloud to your baby on a daily basis.
- Continue to talk to your baby and help your child associate names with corresponding objects.

THE SECOND YEAR

During the second year, babies become toddlers. Sometime in this period they usually begin to walk. They are better able to use their motor skills. They are curious and continue to explore their boundaries and abilities. They begin to assert themselves.

Between the ages of 12 and 24 months, they begin to talk using single words. At that time, they begin using their few words to control their environments; the most popular of these words is "no" (Murphy and Elephant 1974; Hale 1990; MacKain et al. 1983; Oliphant 1975). Sometime during the 12- to 18-month time period, babies usually begin understanding and responding to simple questions. They communicate with a combination of speech and gestures. Most babies know approximately 300 words by the time they are two. Two-years olds understand much of what you say, especially if you speak in clear simple words.

Receptive (heard) vocabulary develops before a child's auditory-kinesthetic-motor abilities are adequate for language production. It is thought that children understand approximately four or five times more than they can verbalize during the 18- to 24-month time period.

There is a difference between a child's receptive lexicon (understanding of words) and his expressive (spoken) vocabulary. For instance, the relationship between these two language functions in an average child might appear as (Locke 1993):

	Begins	Reaches 50 word level
Comprehension (Lexical)	9 months	13 months
Expression (Lexical)	12 months	18 months

Again, it should be kept in mind that there is considerable variation in the normal development of spoken language.

**Suggestions for Stimulating Brain and Language Development
(Adapted from American Academy of Pediatrics 1999)
The Second Year**

- Develop word associations by naming everyday objects and activities.
- Speak slowly and clearly to your child. Give him time to respond.
- Listen and answer your child's questions. Keep answers short and simple.

- Choose books that encourage touching and pointing to objects.
- Read rhymes, jingles, and nursery stories.
- Encourage looking at books and drawings. Discuss these with your child.
- A regular part of the daily routine should be fun, melodic music.
- Be predictable; establish routines for meals, naps, and bedtime.
- Be encouraging and supportive.
- Help your child develop self-control and social awareness by setting appropriate limits.
- Give your child choices. At first, this should be limited to two options.
- Encourage your child to "use your words" to express needs.
- Help your child use words to describe emotions and to express his feelings like happiness, anger, shyness, and fear.
- Help your child to begin to understand "safety" using simple terms.

THE THIRD THROUGH FIFTH YEARS

Physical growth and motor development will slow down somewhat. However, you will observe great changes occurring in intellectual, social, and emotional development. Independence becomes important to a child and he will try to increase his independence from family members. With guidance, the child begins to develop some real self control. The 3- and 4-year-old child will continue to engage in parallel play[8]. As he matures, he will make a transition into cooperative, interactive play.

Usually, children begin stringing words together at about 24 months. Their speech begins to reflect some grammatical patterns. By ages two or three, they begin using three-word phrases and short sentences. Manipulating their tongue, teeth, and lips becomes easier. Their vocabulary increases dramatically. By the time children are three-years old, they should be able to communicate in a fairly purposeful way, asking and answering questions. Both auditory and visual discrimination skills increase as listening and observation increases. During the three- to five-years time, language and speech develop rapidly. Children understand simple questions and begin to understand more complex questions. They ask many questions, but are satisfied with simple answers.

The approximate 80% of children who become fluent in oral language on schedule are apt to learn more information verbally than the 20% of children with language delays. Speaking early produces more response and stimulation from their environment. Thus, nature and nurture work together to prepare a child for the future. It should be remembered that a child who displays difficulty in learning through verbal information may display real strengths in non-verbal abilities and should be taught using other modes of learning such as visual (seeing), kinesthetic (memory of movements), and tactile (touching and feeling).

This is a critical period in language development.[9] By the time children are five years old, they will probably have added the mastery of the pronunciation of the following sounds or phonemes: m, n, ng, f, w, p, h, y, b, d, k, hard g, and all of the vowel sounds to their previously mastered sounds.

Suggestions for Stimulating Brain and Language Development (Adapted from American Academy of Pediatrics 1999) The Third Through Fifth Years

- Encourage creative play. Perhaps find a creative dramatics playgroup.
- Continue building with blocks, Legos, and similar materials.
- Introduce simple construction tools for 5-year-olds.

- Help your child experience creative art activities: finger paint, easel paint, free drawing, and clay.
- Introduce your child to musical instruments. Some research indicates that musical skills can influence math and problem-solving skills. Spend one-to-one personal time with your child.
- Take your child to the grocery store. Name and categorize items as you shop (i.e., "Now, let's buy some vegetables. Corn is a vegetable. What other vegetable should we buy?").
- Offer your child choices when possible. Limit the number of options to two or three.
- Create ways for your child to play with other children.
- Provide social experiences that are outside the home environment.

THE FIFTH THROUGH SEVENTH YEARS

During this period, children's worlds continue to expand rapidly. They are no longer content to be occupied only with themselves and their immediate surroundings, but become conscious and involved with the larger environment. They become aware of being part of "the group." Their large-motor coordination develops rapidly. Small motor development is somewhat slower, but it, too, is developing. Wide spans of differences in motor, speech, and language skills continue to exist.

Their questions have more meaning. They are better able to comprehend answers and continue to ask "why?" Their visual and auditory discriminatory skills are developing; many are getting ready to read. In speech, they usually have mastered the sounds t, l, s, th, zh, v, sh, ch, r, z, and j, if they have not done so earlier.

Suggestions for Stimulating Brain and Language Development
The Fifth through Seventh Years

- That's what this book is all about.
- Please refer to exercises and games in Section I.

CHAPTER 9

Are Your Children Prepared
for Reading Success?

Until recently, children were not required to use graphic symbols until the age of six or seven. Although society has attempted to force the introduction of reading and writing at an earlier age, children's development has demanded delay until they have matured in several ways. At approximately six and a half years of age, most children's central nervous systems are prepared to perceive and associate graphic symbols with previously learned language; in other words, they are ready to learn to read.

Meaningful language must now be associated with what is seen in writing as well as what is heard. The reading process involves the ability to superimpose print symbols on auditory signals; i.e., to associate a spoken word with a sequence of printed letters. Individual differences in this development are present within any group of children and are perfectly normal. Additionally, boys often tend to be somewhat slower in maturation than girls, putting them at additional risk for unreasonable expectations. For that reason, some countries, such as Norway, delay the formal reading and writing process until children are seven-years old, when there is a greater opportunity for success.

PREREQUISITES FOR SUCCESS

To be successful in reading, the child must be able to (1) recognize and recall the sequence of letters within words, (2) tie that particular grouping of visual symbols to its word name, (3) remember how the word sounds and use speech organs to pronounce the word, and (4) connect the word name with previously learned knowledge that helps a child understand the meaning and proper use of the word.

These processes involve much brain activity. Past learning experiences and development of neural pathways have a tremendous effect on the child's success in learning to read.

INSTRUCTION FACTORS TO BE ASSESSED PRIOR TO READING

In assessing readiness for reading, attention should be given to the following factors prior to introducing the reading process. Children can be considered ready for introduction to the complex process of reading with reasonable expectations for success if they:

1) have the general thinking ability of a child who is six and a half[10] or over (the age generally accepted as desirable for "readiness"),
2) are emotionally and socially well balanced,

3) have attained the expected sensory and central nervous system developments,

4) have had adequate language experiences, and

5) have the ability to analyze spoken words into what reading experts call phonemes sounds that are represented by letters (phonological awareness).

Approximately 20% of children have difficulty with sound-symbol associations. These children may see similarities in words, but not relate them to their auditory counterparts. They may also have difficulty relating word parts to the whole word. The most common, directly related reading problem is the delay in developing basic phonological analysis skills. Sounds may not be recognized, coded, organized, stored, and retrieved in an automatic manner. Some of the early warning signs that a child is at risk for specific language processing problems associated with reading difficulties follow.

EARLY SIGNS OF POSSIBLE SPECIFIC LANGUAGE LEARNING DISABILITIES (DYSLEXIA/DYSGRAPHIA)

Difficulty with developing language and learning to talk.
- May be quite delayed compared to other children.
- May have difficulty pronouncing words, misplacing sounds and syllables.
- May be frustrated due to not being able to communicate needs and feelings.
- May have slow vocabulary growth.
- May have difficulty recalling (retrieving) known words.
- May have difficulty in describing something or answering simple questions.
- May have difficulty listening and following directions.
- May have difficulty keeping up with peer group activities; depends upon observation of their actions rather than verbal communication.
- May continuously mispronounce words.
- May not talk in sentences by three to four years of age.
- May have difficulty learning letters or numbers as compared to other children of the same age.
- May have difficulty in associating known letter symbols (graphemes) with spoken sounds (phonemes).

OTHER DIFFICULTIES OFTEN ASSOCIATED WITH SPECIFIC LANGUAGE LEARNING DISABILITIES

These may include one or more of the following:

- May have difficulty in sustaining interest in hearing stories.
- May demonstrate poor coordination and will avoid certain activities such as using crayons, pencils and/or scissors.
- May seem impulsive, and have difficulty sustaining attention during certain activities such as watching a video, completing a project, or listening to discussions.

Children who are at risk for specific language disabilities may exhibit any combination of the above characteristics. At-risk children should be identified prior to allowing them to suffer failure, embarrassment, and frustration. Instruments such as the Slingerland Pre-Reading Screening Tests, and other indepth testing by qualified personnel have been shown to be effective in identifying these risk factors. Upon identification as being "at risk" for reading and written language success, further appropriate multisensory strategies such as the Slingerland or Orton-Gillingham based approaches should be initiated as soon as possible.[11]

The exercises and games found in this book will assist all children in building a strong language foundation. This language foundation is necessary for successful reading and written language skills. A child who does not have a language learning disability will profit from these activities, instead of having language development left to haphazard learning. This instruction is vital for children who are at risk for language learning disabilities. Their future success depends upon building a solid language foundation.

Section III
Support Materials

CHAPTER 10

Preparing Materials for Instruction

PICTURE FOLDERS

- Assemble some 24 folders, each to contain pictures needed for use in some of the exercises and games.
- Number each folder and number the pictures to correspond to the folders for quick and easy filing.
- Mount pictures on uniform size cards, approximately 9x11 inches. Strong tagboard is advised.
- Pictures can be obtained from magazines, old books, and catalogs as well as from other sources. Be on the lookout for pictures at all times.
- Pictures should be large enough to be seen with ease by children sitting in a group, and the children should be seated so that they do not view the pictures from too sharp an angle.
- Good taste should be followed in picture selection, and advertisements should be removed. Children prefer color pictures but clearly defined black and whites are useful also.
- The pictures to be collected, mounted, and kept in the numbered folders will be used to illustrate the names of objects and to help children associate visual images with the language needed to express the ideas and concepts called forth.
- These pictures should not be used for display about the room or left in the hands of the children. They are used only during the lesson time and put away when not in actual use.

Tagboard folders made by you, or large envelopes found in stationery and bookstores, serve as individual containers for each set of pictures. If you make the folders, I suggest folding the lower and upper edges of the folders to form pockets that prevent pictures from falling out.

DIRECTIONS FOR ASSEMBLING PICTURE FOLDERS

FOLDER 1 *Pictures to build vocabulary*
The pictures should show some activity such as: children making cookies, children playing together, a family looking at something, a child drawing, children in the snow.

Suitable pictures are most likely to be found in full-page advertisements in large magazines.

FOLDER 2 *Matching pictures*
The pictures should be in duplicate sets, each exactly alike, and should be appealing to children such as: a child with a birthday cake, clowns, children on a merry-go-round, children playing, children eating.

FOLDERS 3, 4, 5, 6, 7, 8 Vocabulary—classification

The pictures are for building vocabulary and an understanding of classification.

> *FOLDER 3 Pictures of wild animals such as elephants, kangaroos, lions, leopards, deer, bears, or giraffes.*

> *FOLDER 4 Pictures of domestic animals such as horses, cows, sheep, pigs, dogs, or cats.*

> *FOLDER 5 Pictures of things to ride in or on such as automobiles, airplanes, tricycles, bicycles, wagons, coasters, horses, carts, canoes, freighters, passenger ships, baby buggies, sailboats, or scooters.*

> *FOLDER 6 Pictures of foods such as bread, cake, meat, turkeys, chicken pie, different vegetables, fruit, berries, or bacon.*

> *FOLDER 7 Pictures of buildings such as houses, churches, buildings (offices, warehouses, sky-scrapers, banks), apartment houses, or schools.*

> *FOLDER 8 Pictures of workers such as police officers, firefighters, bakers, bankers, truck drivers, pharmacists, carpenters, engineers, pilots, bus drivers, doctors, or clerks in stores and fast food restaurants.*

FOLDER 9 Picture cards to build vocabulary and concept

The pictures should be small enough to fit on cards made of manila tagboard, approximately 4x5.5 inches. Take care in keeping pictures large enough, however, to be seen by a child or small group of children without eyestrain. Provide a large number of cards, a hundred or more, on which are pictures of things familiar to children, such as vegetables, parts of the body, fruits, musical instruments, toys, clothing, people, tools, furniture, cooking utensils, things to ride in or on, flowers, buildings, or animals.

FOLDER 10 Pictures for contrasts and resemblances in complex situations

The pictures should be of farm scenes and city scenes, such as children on a country road and a city street, vehicle with a country background and with a city background, farm scenes and city traffic, children playing in hay and playing in a city park, or fishing in a stream and skyscraper scene. Other sets of contrasting pictures may be of day and night, forest and desert, winter and summer, or work and play.

FOLDER 11 Pictures that lend themselves to use of prepositional phrases

The pictures should show something in a dish, on the table, by the wall, outside the barn, under the house, inside the box, on the tree, for a child, over the house, or to take away.

FOLDER 12 Pictures that lend themselves to use of adjectives

The pictures should be of something that can be described as:

big	little
large	small
long	short
high	low
happy	sad
thick	thin
rainy	cloudy
merry	sunny
happy	sleepy
pretty	healthy
beautiful	busy

kind	strong
sad	sickly

Suggested pictures for color adjectives:

tall skyscrapers	a low stool
a high shelf	big elephants
a round ball	a scary witch
some little boys	fat pumpkins
pretty dresses	bright stars

FOLDER 13 Singular and plural

The pictures should be of objects to show singular and plural, such as:

clock	clocks
house	houses
puppy	puppies
banana	bananas
apple	apples
boy	boys
child	children

FOLDER 14 Sets have pictures illustrating incidents in a story

Sets of pictures can be found in inexpensive booklets sold in variety stores or in discarded pre-reading workbooks.

FOLDER 15 Pictures to promote thought

The pictures should be thought-provoking, such as:

a family at the zoo looking through bars at something in a cage

a family picnic on the beach (or in the forest)

someone delivering or bringing home groceries and placing them on a table

a child opening a package

FOLDER 16 Pictures to use in reproducing a story

Sets of pictures, each set to illustrate the story sequence of a familiar tale such as *The Three Bears*, *Yertle the Turtle*, or *Curious George* are needed. Variety stores sell inexpensive books carrying large illustrations. It is usually necessary to purchase two copies of each booklet if the pictures are on both sides of the same leaf, since they are to be cut out and each mounted on separate cards.

FOLDER 17 Pictures to give two aspects of the same idea

The pictures should be in pairs consisting of pictures giving the same idea or showing the same action (but not duplicates), such as:

A child drinking milk	A child drinking orange juice
A family having a turkey dinner	A family having a picnic
A child looking at a book	Some children looking at books
A clown	Another clown in different makeup

FOLDER 18 Pictures of single objects

The pictures should be of single objects, preferably without backgrounds, such as:

Bicycle, stove, horse, cat, doll, bucket, ball, ship, roast, chair, blocks, bed, sink

FOLDER 19 Pictures for rhyme and visual association

The pictures should be of single objects, the names of which lend themselves to rhyming, and there should be as little background as possible. Suggestions for pictures with rhyming words:

dog	hog, log
house	mouse
boy	toy
girl	curl, pearl
box	socks, fox, clocks
tree	bee, sea, flea
sun	fun, bun, nun
flower	tower, shower
kitten	mitten
bed	bread, head, thread
man	pan, fan
train	rain, stain, brain
toaster	roaster, coaster

FOLDER 20 Geometric plane figures

The figures should be made in duplicate. Six or seven sets are better.

Figures for use should be:

Square	approximately 6 inches
Triangle	approximately 6 inches
Circle	approximately 6 inches in diameter
Rectangle	approximately 6 x 9 inches

The figures should be cut from sturdy tagboard or something of durable composition.

FOLDER 21 Linear drawings

On cards approximately 6 x 9 inches, draw the following figures with a felt pen:

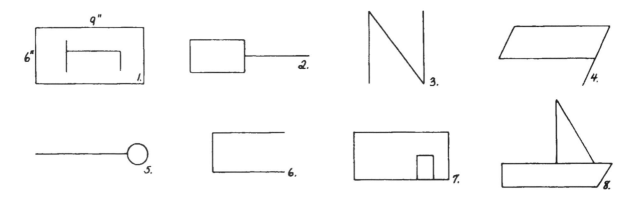

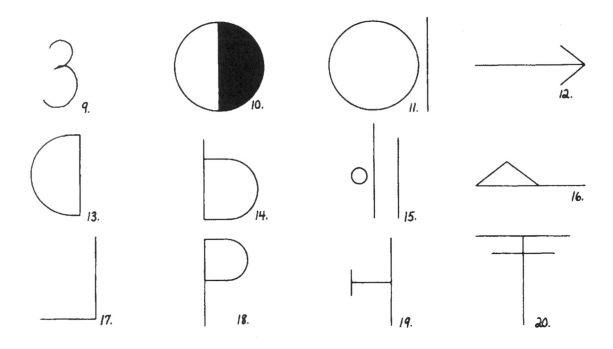

FOLDER 22 *Pattern cards to use with rhythms*

To make these pattern cards, use 12-inch strips of tagboard.

The pattern is shown on the card by attaching large and small colored dot stickers or large and small Xs to show pattern. The "rest" sign is shown as a vertical line: "|".

The count is as in 4/4 time in music; that is, each section should have four counts with a whole note receiving one count. The half-notes (in this case, the small items) receive 1/2 counts.

The large figures each receive one count while clapping or tapping rhythms. The small figures each receive 1/2 count. When children see the rests, they should turn rhythm sticks or their wrists out away from their bodies to indicate the rest. (The words and numbers are included here as a "help" to the teacher. They should not be included on the pattern cards.)

Examples of suggested patterns for Folder 22 to use with rhythms

0	0	|	|		
long	long	long	long		
(count:)	1	2	3	4	

|	|o	o	|	|	
long	short	short	long	long	
1	2	"and"	3	4	

|	Ω	|	Ω		
long	long rest	long	long rest		
1	2	3	4		

|	Ω	o	o	Ω	
long	long rest	short	short	long rest	
1	2	3	"and"	4	

o	o	|	o	o	Ω
short	short	long	short	short	long rest
1	"and"	2	3	"and"	4

|	o	o	|	/	/
long	short	short	long	short rest	short rest
1	2	"and"	3	4	"and"

FOLDER 23 Picture cards with a single object

Paste pictures on back of 3x5 cards. Pictures may be found in magazines, catalogs, and old readiness books. If you prefer, these cards may be purchased from a school supply store or the Ideal School Supply Co., Oak Lawn, Illinois 60453.

FOLDER 24 Double set of picture or pattern cards

Two sets of cards that are exactly alike are used in the memory game. Cards may be made using index cards with stickers, pictures from old readiness books, or geometric forms. Commercially prepared "Concentration Memory" cards are relatively inexpensive, as are playing cards.

BOXES OF OBJECTS OR SMALL TOYS

Small objects and toys to be used during some of the lesson periods may be found in dime stores, toy shops, or in the home. Like the pictures, do not leave them for display or where children can play with them during free time. The following are suggested groups of objects that have been found to be available and useful. These groups of items may be used interchangeably for activities calling for Box 1. Keeping these groups in smaller containers will make it easy to choose items to vary the activities and maintain the children's interest. Some need to be provided in duplicate sets.

BOX 1
- *Doll's knife, fork, and spoon*
- *Plastic hoe, rake, and spade*
- *Small plastic, metal, or wooden animals—dog, horse, cow, cat, sheep, lion, giraffe, etc.*
- *Pencil, eraser, slate, ruler, and small book*

- *Small pieces of velvet, satin, net, sponge, sandpaper, wood, bar of iron, and stick of wood*
- *Small hammer, saw, nail, screw, screwdriver, and scissors*
- *Toy watch, bottle, toothbrush, comb, dish, plate, cup, and toy eggbeater*
- *Small model of an automobile, carriage, sled, airplane, truck, and boat*
- *Geometrical plane figures—square, rectangle, circle, and triangle*
- *Geometrical solid figures—sphere, cube, cone, cylinder, and pyramid*
- *Thimble, spool of thread*
- *Small paintbrushes, small plastic boxes*
- *Colored cubes, plastic disks, buttons and/or other game markers*

BOX 2 Identical sets of small objects and toys

There should be two of each, exactly alike.

For use with visual recall.

BOX 3

Small wooden cubes, plastic disks, wooden beads, or other markers. Collection should contain a minimum of five colors. Inexpensive sets can be made by spray painting lima beans.

There should be a minimum of 36 to be divided among a group of six children.

Adaptive   Develops or changes to meet requirements of the environment. The reorganization of the brain based on selective experience.

Anomia   The loss of memory of the pronunciation of the name of a word. The inability to retrieve the name of a word even though the individual may recognize it and understand the concept.

Apoptosis   The process in which extraneous neurons are pruned (removed) due to lack of stimulation and use.

Association   A connection between ideas or items; i.e., letters and sounds.

Axon   The output system of the neural cell. The axon carries the messages from the neural cell, through the dendrites (input system) of another cell.

Auditory   Information processed from hearing.

Auditory comprehension   The ability to understand the concepts embedded in information that is heard.

Auditory discrimination   Being able to notice and recognize the difference between two or more sounds.

Auditory recall (memory)   Being able to remember information that has been heard, and to retrieve that information on demand. This requires adequate reception, storage, and retrieval of auditorily presented information.

Auditory sequencing   The ability to recall, in the proper sequence, information that has been heard.

Blending   A process of combining or blending phonemes (sounds) together to synthesize phonetic words. The techniques for blending require hearing the word (either externally or internally), the segmentation of phonemes (sounds), and their associations with their corresponding graphemes (letters). In the Slingerland Approach, the word "blending" is sometimes used synonymously with the term encoding as a part of spelling. In recent years, the term "blending" is also being used in the process of "decoding." This begins at the opposite end of the processing, first seeing and recognizing the graphemes (letters), then associating the phonemes (sounds), and finally putting these sounds together to pronounce or read the word.

Breve   The curved diacritical mark placed above a vowel to indicate that the vowel sound is short.

Capitals or capital letters   Uppercase manuscript or cursive letters.

Cardiac deceleration   A slowing of the heart beat.

Comprehension   The ability to extract meaning from either listening (auditory stimulus) or written print (visual stimulus).

Decoding   The techniques required in identifying word parts and then whole words. The graphemes (letters) and syllables in a word are segmented. The grapheme-phoneme correspondences are then synthesized into spoken or read words.

Dendrites   Small extensions of the neurons that receive information from other nerve cells through synaptic connections (synapses).

Discrimination   The ability to distinguish similarities and differences between items.
- visual discrimination, in reading, refers to the ability to visually distinguish similarities and differences in letters and words that are graphically similar.
- auditory discrimination, the ability to distinguish similarities and differences within sounds and words by listening.

Digraph   A consonant digraph is a combination of two adjacent consonants that express a single sound, such as ck in jack, ch in chair, th in thimble, th in this (voiced sound), sh in ship, and wh in wheel.

A vowel diagraph is a combination of two adjacent vowels that express a single vowel sound as ee in meet, oa in boat, or ea in head.

Dyslexia   "Dyslexia is a neurologically based, often familial, disorder which interferes with the acquisition and processing of language. Varying in degrees of severity, it is manifested by difficulties in receptive and expressive language, including phonological processing, in reading, writing, spelling, handwriting, and sometimes in arithmetic. Dyslexia is not a result of lack of motivation, sensory impairment, inadequate instructional or environmental opportunities, or other limiting conditions, but may occur together with these conditions. Although dyslexia is life-long, individuals with dyslexia frequently respond successfully to timely and appropriate intervention." (Committee of Members, Orton Dyslexia Society 1994.)

Another definition of dyslexia is a difficulty in learning to process written language. Studies have indicated a neurological basis for this disorder.

Electroencephalogram (electrophysiological procedures)   These non-invasive electrophysiological procedures are used to indicate synaptic activity or background electrical activity that is a by-product of neuronal communication. According to Nelson and Bloom (1998), it is very sensitive to state changes and perhaps underlying changes in emotionality.

Embedded   Set within an enclosing mass. In language, it could refer to a sound within a word, a word within a sentence, or an idea within a selection.

Encoding   Translating sounds into symbols. In the Slingerland Approach, the word "encoding" is sometimes used synonymously with "blending." Encoding requires the segmentation of phonemes and their association with their corresponding graphemes, which is necessary in order to spell words. This process is opposite to the process of decoding, which begins with the visual symbols and is required for reading. (*See* Decoding.)

Environmental   All of the conditions and circumstances surrounding and affecting the development of an organism.

Expressive vocabulary   Words that one is able to say or write in the correct context.

Genetic   The inheritable factors (genes) that shape the biological development of an organism.

Glial cells   Cells found within the central nervous system (CNS) that provide structural support in networks of nerves. Some of these cells form the myelin sheaths around the axons that allow neural signals/information to be transmitted more rapidly. Some of the other activities include providing support functions for neurons such as guiding developing neurons to the correct locations within the brain, storing extra energy for active neurons, and complementing the neurons in certain metabolic activities. At birth, the brain contains one trillion glial cells (American Academy of Pediatrics 1999).

Grapheme   The graphic symbol, a single letter (or sometimes more than one letter) that represents a single sound (phoneme).

In Utero   The time period when the fetus is developing within the uterus.

Keyword   A word used to assist memory in recalling the phoneme that is represented by a grapheme, for example using a picture of a turtle to recall the sound for the letter t.

Kinesthetic   In the Slingerland Approach, kinesthetic refers to the automatic memory of the sequence of movements necessary to direct the motor movements for speech and handwriting.

Learning disability   Unusual difficulty in learning an academic skill at a level that would be expected in relation to the individual's level of intelligence and other skills. This may be present in only one area or may affect several areas of learning. The legal definition, as found in the EHA, 20 U.S.C.ß 1401 (15), is:

The term "children with specific learning disabilities" means those children who have a disorder in one or more of the basic psychological processes involved in understanding or in using language, spoken or written, which disorder may manifest itself in imperfect ability to listen, think, speak, read, write, spell, or do mathematical calculations. Such disorders include such conditions as perceptual handicaps, brain injury, minimal brain dysfunction, dyslexia, and developmental aphasia. Such term does not include children who have learning problems which are primarily the result of visual, hearing, or motor handicaps, of mental retardation, of emotional disturbance, or of environmental, cultural, or economic disadvantage.

Letter recognition   The ability to recognize and point out the symbol for a named letter. The ability to name a letter when shown its symbol. (These are two different processes.)

Literacy   The ability to read and write at a level that allows effective functioning.

Manuscript handwriting   Manuscript handwriting is often referred to as printing. Letters are formed as independent units that are not connected.

Memory   Involves the reception, storage, and retrieval of sensory information.
- Short-term memory refers to immediate, limited memory that lasts only briefly.
- Long-term memory refers to more lasting memory which is stored within the brain for later recall.
- Auditory memory refers to the reception, storage, and retrieval of auditorily presented information. In language, this includes phonemes, spoken words, and spoken language.
- Visual memory refers to the reception, storage, and retrieval of visually presented information. In language, this usually includes letters, words, phrases, or formulas.

Monosyllable   One syllable, from the Greek *mono* meaning one.

Morpheme   A meaningful linguistic unit that contains no smaller meaningful parts, such as the trigraph <u>tch</u>, base words, affixes, and roots.

Morphology   The study of the structure of words that includes morphemes.

Multisensory   The use of auditory (hearing), kinesthetic-motor (feeling), and visual (seeing) channels to reinforce learning.

Myelination   The wrapping of the axons with a fatty-like substance that insulates the cell and allows the axons to conduct information more efficiently (American Academy of Pediatrics 1999). This lipid and protein substance is produced from Schwann cells (a type of glial cell).

Neurons   These cells are the basic building blocks of the brain. At birth, the brain contains 100 billion neurons. The brain is developed through the organization, connective, and specialization processes of the neurons and glial cells.

Neural   Pertaining to the structure of the brain and its components.

Neural plasticity   The ability of the brain to be shaped and/or changed by experience which, in turn, allows for new experiences, thus leading to further neural changes. Within limits, this reorganization of the brain, based on experience, can occur throughout life.

Neurotransmitters or neuromodulators   Chemical signals that pass information through a circuit of neurons. Neurotransmitters or neuromodulators facilitate this activity by passing from the axon of one cell to the dendrites of another neural cell. They may also facilitate the formation of new synapses.

Non-nutritive sucking   The sucking activity without the presence of a substance.

Nonsense word   This is a word that has no real meaning; however, it looks like a real word because of its pattern or type. Nonsense words are useful when teaching elementary decoding skills because students will not recognize them and will be compelled to apply their decoding techniques.

Nurture   Experiences provided by the environment.

Perception   The ability to isolate, identify, and organize a specific stimulus among several stimuli. In the Slingerland Approach, perception is a pre-blending auditory exercise where students are required to identify the vowel phonemes and graphemes in words.

Phoneme   A sound. One of the smallest bits of speech that distinguishes one utterance from another as /b/ in ball and /oi/ in boy. English comprises approximately 45 phonemes or sounds.

Phonemic awareness   "The understanding that spoken words and syllables are made up of sequences of speech elements. This understanding of the structure of language is necessary for learning to read or spell an alphabetic language, such as English, because letters represent the elements. It requires the ability to recognize, combine, and manipulate sound units. Phonics will make no sense unless there is phonemic awareness" (Murray 2002).

Phonemic segmentation   The act of segmenting or separating out individual sounds from clusters of sounds.

Phonological awareness   "The ability to attend to the sounds of speech in language. Phonological awareness is a more inclusive term than phonemic awareness. Indications of this awareness include noticing similar sounds in words, appreciating rhymes and counting syllables" (Hall and Moats 1999).

Phonics   A reading and spelling approach to teaching literacy skills that focuses on phoneme-grapheme correspondences.

Phonetics   The study and systematic classification of speech sounds, including auditory perception, articulation, and acoustics (Murray 2002).

Phonogram   Slingerland defined a phonogram as a vowel digraph (ee or ay), a diphthong (a speech sound made by gliding from one vowel to another, such as oi in oil). For convenience and simplicity in use, Slingerland includes all the vowel digraphs and diphthongs as well as the v-e syllable that technically are not phonograms. More traditionally, a phonogram is defined as a group of letters that usually represents the same sound or phonemes, such as igh and ee (Murray 2002).

Plasticity   Malleability. *see* Neural Plasticity.

Pre-natal   Prior to birth.

Pruning (apoptosis)   The process that the brain uses to remove extraneous neural connections and/or speech sounds. During the first year of life, there is an overproduction of synapses. A pruning or the elimination of extraneous neurons follows this. These neurons are those that are not stimulated and reinforced through use.

Receptive vocabulary   The understanding of information that one receives through sight or sound.

Retrieval   The ability to recall, on demand, the word name or other information that has been learned or heard at a previous time.

Sibilant   A speech sound such as /s/, /z/, /sh/, /zh/, and /ch/. These are often difficult for the kindergarten aged child due to the loss of front teeth.

Sound-symbol association   (Also referred to as sound-letter association and/or phoneme-grapheme association.) The correspondence or connection between the letter (graphic symbol) and the speech sound (phoneme).

Specific language disability   *See* the synonymous definition for dyslexia.

Stimulate   To rouse to action.

Syllable   A unit of spoken language consisting of an uninterrupted utterance and forming either a whole word (stomp) or a commonly recognized division of a word (cat/nip).

Syllabification   The process of dividing or breaking words into separate syllables usually for decoding or encoding and spelling.

Synaptogenesis   The formation of synapses that connect the axons of the sending neuron to the dendrites of the receiving neuron.

Voiced sounds   Sounds in speech that requires the vibration of the vocal chords for their production (/th/ as in the word this, /v/ as in the word vase).

Voiceless or unvoiced sounds   Consonant sounds that are made without vibration of the vocal chords when produced. (/th/ as in the word thimble, /p/ as in the word pig).

Vowels   Letters of the alphabet which represent sounds or phonemes that open the throat or are voiced and unobstructed. In English, the "short" vowels are a, e, i, o, u, and sometimes y and w. The y is a vowel when it acts as i's twin; it is a consonant usually at the beginning of words and syllables and when pronounced /y/; w acts as a vowel when it does not have its consonant sound /w/ and usually as u's twin in phonograms such as <u>aw</u>, <u>er</u>, and <u>ow</u>. Traditionally, each of the common vowels has a short and long sound. Short vowels are typically found in monosyllabic words (had, bed, inch, lot, cut) or in accented closed syllables (ap/ple, el/e/phant, In/di/an, ol/ives, um/brel/la). Long vowels usually occur at the end of monosyllabic words (me, hi, no) or at the end of accented, open syllables ba/by, me/ter, ti/ger, po/ny, tu/lip) (Murray 2002).

Visual   Processing information that is received through sight.

Visual discrimination   In language, visual discrimination refers to the ability to distinguish visually (see) similarities and differences between and among letters and in words.

Visual comprehension   The ability to understand an item that has been seen, particularly as it pertains to reading.

Visual memory or recall   Visual memory refers to the reception, storage, and retrieval of visually presented information. In language, visual memory includes graphemes, words, and text.

Visual perception   The ability to recognize and organize visual images.

Visual recall   The ability to retrieve, or call back from memory, the image of the item that has been seen.

Visual sequencing   Recalling the exact order of items that have been seen.

1 For further information, contact the Slingerland Institute for Literacy, One Bellevue Center, 411 108th Ave. N.E., Bellevue, WA 98004. Phone: (425)-453-1190. Fax: (425)-635-7762. E-mail: SlingInst@aol.com. Web site: www.slingerland.org.

2 Raising thumbs assists the teacher in assessment while avoiding the problem of children receiving wrong cues from other children. It also prevents embarrassment for the children who do not yet recognize rhymes.

3 Keyword Cards and other Slingerland materials are available from Educator's Publishing Service, www.epsbooks.com.

4 Thanks go to Yolanda Piziali, a Slingerland-trained Santa Barbara kindergarten teacher, for this idea.

5 Cautionary notes regarding expectations of children's writing should not be interpreted as directions to stop a child from voluntarily writing small letters. Remember, some children are developmentally ready earlier than their peers. The teacher should be observing closely and individualizing instructions for these children.

6 word-call: the ability to say words while lacking the understanding of concepts or meaning of the whole

7 stimulus-response: trained to respond to a certain stimulus in a specific way, regardless of comprehension

8 parallel play: children engaging in the same type of activity, but playing side by side rather than cooperatively

9 If the child doesn't appear to be developing basic, meaningful, age-appropriate communication skills, contact your physician or the nearest children's hospital for a referral to a speech and language specialist for an evaluation. In most states, this service is provided by the public school system at the age of three and above. If your child should have a language learning disability, it is important to have a professional evaluation and begin any needed language therapy as soon as possible.

10 In the educational and psychological literature, this is often expressed as "mental age."

11 The Slingerland multisensory approach to language arts is a classroom adaptation of the Orton-Gillingham multisensory approach. It may be used in regular education classrooms with small groups or individuals. The Slingerland Institute for Literacy provides teachers with effective instructional tools for working with students ranging from kindergarten through

adulthood. For more information on this training, as well as information regarding the advanced classes, contact The Slingerland Institute for Literacy (a non-profit teacher-education agency). Slingerland Institute for Literacy, One Bellevue Center, 411 108th Ave. N.E., Bellevue, WA 98004, www.slingerland.org.

Aaron, P. G., and Joshi, R. M. 1992. *Reading Problems: Consultation and Remediation.* New York: Guilford Press.

American Academy of Pediatrics. 1999. AAP early brain and child development presentation kit. Early Brain and Child Development (EBCD) Project Advisory and Planning group and the faculty from the EBCD Workshop in Houston.

Ball, E. W., and Blackman, B. A. 1991. Does phonemic awareness training in kindergarten make a difference in early word recognition and developmental spelling? *Reading Research Quarterly* 26:49–66.

Bender, L. 1957. Specific reading disability as a maturational lag. *Bulletin of The Orton Society* 7:9–18.

Benedict, H. 1979. Early lexical development: Comprehension and production. *Journal of Child Language* 6:183–200.

Calfee, R. C., Lindamood, P. E., and Lindamood, C. H. 1973. Acoustic-phonetic skills and reading: Kindergarten through 12th grade. *Journal of Educational Psychology* 64:293–298.

DeCasper, A., and Fifer, W. P. 1980. On human bonding: Newborns prefer their mothers' voices. *Science* 1174–6.

Dodd, B.1972. Effects of social and vocal stimulation on infant babbling. *Developmental Psychology* 7:80–83.

Dozier, P. 1953. The neurological background of word deafness. *Bulletin of The Orton Society* 3:6–9.

Eilers, R. E., and Minifie, F. D. 1975. Fricative discrimination in early infancy. *Journal of Speech and Hearing Research* 18:158–67.

Eisenson, J. 1958. Aphasia and dyslexia in children. *Bulletin of The Orton Society* 8:3–8.

Epstein, H. 1978. Growth spurts during brain development: Implications for educational policy and practice. In *Education and the Brain*, eds. J. Chall and H. Mirsky. Seventy-fifth Yearbook of the National Society for the Study of Education (Part 11). Chicago: NSSE.

Felton, B. H., and Pepper, P. P. 1995. Early identification and intervention of phonological deficits in kindergarten and early elementary children at risk for reading disability. *School Psychology Review* 24:405–14.

Foorman, B. R., Francis, D. J., Shaywitz, S. E., Shaywitz, B. A., and Fletcher, J. M. 1997. The case for early reading interventions. In *Foundations of Reading Acquisition and Dyslexia: Implications for Early Intervention*, ed. B. Blachman. Mahwah, NJ: Lawrence Erlbaum Associates.

Foorman, B. R., Francis, D. J., Beeler, T., Winikates, D., and Fletcher, J. M. 1997. Early interventions for children with reading problems. *Scientific Studies of Reading* 1:255–276.

Gillingham, A. 1949 (Nov.). Avoiding failure in reading and spelling. *Independent School Bulletin.*

Gillingham, A. 1951 (Jan.). The language function. *Independent School Bulletin.*

Gillingham, A. 1955 (Apr.). The obligation of the school to teach reading and spelling. *Independent School Bulletin.*

Hale, M. 1990. Oral presentation to Slingerland Institute for Literacy. Seattle, WA.

Hall, S., and Moats, L. 1999. *Straight Talk about Reading.* Lincolnwood, IL: Contemporary Books.

Healy, J. M. 1990. *Endangered Minds: Why Our Children Don't Think.* New York: Simon & Schuster.

Healy, J. M. 1987. *Your Child's Growing Mind.* Garden City, NY: Doubleday & Co.

Hermann, K. 1959. *Reading Disability: A Medical Study of Word Blindness and Related Handicaps.* Springfield, IL: Charles C Thomas.

de Hirsch, K. 1957. Tests designed to discover potential reading difficulties at the six-year-old level. *American Journal of Orthopsychiatry* 27:566–76.

de Hirsch, K. 1953. Developmental word deafness and speech therapy. *Bulletin of The Orton Society* 3:11–20.

de Hirsch, K.1962. Psychological correlates of the reading process. Challenge and Experiment in Reading, *International Reading Association* 218–25.

Kuhl, P. K., and Meltzoff, A. N. 1982. The bimodal perception of speech in infancy. *Science* 218:1138–41.

Langford, W. E. 1955. Developmental dyspraxia-abnormal clumsiness. *Bulletin of The Orton Society* 5:3–8.

Lecanuet, J. P., Granier-Deferre, C., and Busnel, M. C. 1989. Differential fetal auditory responses: Reactiveness as a function of stimulus characteristics and state. *Seminars in Perinatology* 13: 421–29.

Lieberman, I. Y. 1973. Segmentation of the spoken word and reading acquisition. *Bulletin of The Orton Society* 23:65–77.

Lieberman, I. Y., Shankweiler, D., Fischer, F. W., and Carter B. 1974. Explicit syllable and phoneme segmentation in the young child. *Journal of Experimental Child Psychology* 18: 201–212.

Lieberman, I. Y. 1985. Linguistic abilities and spelling proficiency in kindergartners and adult poor spellers. In *Biobehavioral Measures of Dyslexia*, eds. D. B. Gray and J. F. Kavanagh, Parkton, MD: York Press.

Lindbloom, B. 1989. Some remarks on the origin of the phonetic code. In *Brain and Reading*, eds. C. M. Euler, I. Lundberg, and G. Lennerstrand. New York: Stockton Press.

Lindamood, C., and Lindamood, P. 1975. *The A.D.D. Program: Auditory Discrimination in Depth.* Austin, TX: PRO-ED.

Locke, J. L. 1993. *The Child's Path to Spoken Language.* Cambridge, MA: Harvard University Press.

MacKain, K. S. 1983. Speaking without a tongue. *Journal of the National Student Speech Language Hearing Association* 12:46–71.

Meltzoff, A. N. 1986. Imitation, intermodal representation, and the origins of mind. In *Precursors of Early Speech*, eds. B. Lindblom and R. Zetterstrom. New York: Stockton Press.

Molfese, D. L., Freeman, R. B., and Palermo, D. S. 1975. The ontogeny of brain lateralization for speech and nonspeech stimuli. *Brain and Language* 2:356–368.

Money, J. 1962. Dyslexia: A post conference review. In *Reading Disability, Progress and Research Needs in Dyslexia*, ed. John Money. Baltimore: Johns Hopkins Press.

Monroe, M. 1932. *Children Who Cannot Read.* Chicago: University of Chicago Press.

Moon, C., and Fifer, W. P. 1988. Newborn response to a male voice. Paper presented at the International Conference on Infant Studies, April 21–24, Washington, D.C.

Moon, C., and Fifer, W. P. 1990. Syllables as signals for 2-day-old infants. *Infant Behavior and Development* 13:377–390.

Murray, C. 2002. *Scope and Sequence for Literacy Instruction.* 2nd Editon. Baltimore, MD: York Press.

Nelson, C. A. 2000. The neurobiological bases of early intervention in print. In *Handbook of Early Child Intervention* (2nd edition), eds. S. J. Meisels and J. P. Shonkoff. Cambridge, MA: University Press.

Nelson, C. A., and Bloom, F. E. 1998 (Oct.). Child development and neuroscience. *Child Development* 68:970–987.

Nelson, C. A. 1999. *Neural Plasticity and Human Development.* American Pyschological Society. Blackwell Publishers, Inc. Maldon, MA.

Oliphant, G. 1972. *Alphabet Alchemy.* Cambridge, MA: Educators Publishing Service, Inc.

Oliphant, G. 1975. Personal Communication.

Orton, S. T. 1934 (Nov.). The development of speech understanding in relation to intelligence. Lecture delivered at the Woods School Institute. Langhorne, PA.

Orton, S. T. 1937. *Reading, Writing and Speech Problems in Children.* New York: W. W. Norton & Co.

Penfield, W. 1964. The uncommitted cortex. *Atlantic Monthly* 214:77–82.

Piaget, J., and Inhelder, B. 1969. *The Psychology of the Child.* New York: Basic Books, Inc.

Premack, D. 1972. Two problems in cognition: Symbolization, and from icon to phoneme. In *Communication and Effect: A Comparative Approach*, eds. T. Alloway, L. Krames, and P. Pliner. New York: Academic Press.

Rosner, J. 1993. *Helping Children Overcome Learning Difficulties.* New York: Walker & Co.

Shaywitz, S. E. 1998 (Jan. 29). Dyslexia. *The New England Journal of Medicine* 338:307–12.

Slingerland, B. H. 1967. *Training in Some Prerequisites for Beginning Reading.* Cambridge, MA: Educators Publishing Service, Inc.

Slingerland, B. H. 1994. *A Multi-Sensory Approach to Language Arts for Specific Language Disability Children: A Guide for Elementary Teachers.* Cambridge, MA: Educators' Publishing Service, Inc.

Slingerland B. H. 1996. *A Multi-Sensory Approach to Language Arts for Specific Language Disability Children: A Guide for Primary Teachers.* Cambridge, MA: Educators' Publishing Service, Inc.

Slingerland, B. H., and Aho, M. 1985a. *Learning to Use Manuscript Handwriting.* Cambridge, MA: Educators Publishing Service, Inc.

Slingerland, B. H., and Aho, M. 1985c. *Learning to Use Cursive Handwriting.* Cambridge, MA: Educators Publishing Service, Inc.

Slingerland B. H., and Murray C. 1987. *Teachers' Word Lists for Reference*, Revised Edition. Cambridge, MA: Educators' Publishing Service, Inc.

Stanovich, K. E. 1986. Matthew effects in reading: Some consequences of individual differences in the acquisition of literacy. *Reading Research Quarterly* 21:360–406.

Strunk, D. 1982. Personal Communication. University of San Diego, CA.

Torgesen, J. K. 1993. Phonological awareness: A critical factor in dyslexia. A brochure from *The Orton Emeritus Series*, The International Dyslexia Association.

Vail, P. L. 1994. *Emotion: The On/Off Switch for Learning.* Rosemont, NJ: Modern Learning Press.

Vail, P. L. 1992. *Learning Styles.* Rosemont, NJ: Modern Learning Press.

Vail, P. L. 1991. *Common Ground: Whole Language and Phonics Working Together.* Rosemont, NJ: Modern Learning Press.

Vail, P. L. 1987. *Smart Kids With School Problems: Things to Know and Ways to Help.* New York: Penguin Books.

Wepman, J. M. 1962. Dyslexia: Its relationship to language acquisition and concept formation. Reading Disability, Progress and Research Needs. In *Dyslexia*, ed. John Money. Baltimore: Johns Hopkins Press.

Obervation, promoting thought based on, 21
Omission game, 55, 60, 69
Omitted units of sounds, 51–52; from compound words, 53–57; from words with suffixes, 57–59; from words with syllables, 59–60
Oral expression, activities to assist in, 89–94
Oral language, 4; importance of, 121; reading and, 2
Oral reading, requirements for, 2

P

Pacing of lessons, 78
Parent and child, attachment between, 125
Pencil, guidance to properly hold a, 74
Phoneme, the least common (in the world), 128
Phoneme-grapheme association, discrimination of letters and, 79
Phonemes, 30: at the beginning of names, 40; at the beginning of words, 39–40, 61–62; discriminating between, 38–39, 63–64; discrimination of specified initial, 42–43; at the end of words, 41–42, 62; omitting, 60–61, 68–70; recognizing embedded, 61–62; recognizing and manipulating individual, 53, 65–68, 71–72; recognizing the number of (in a word), 63–65, 71; recognizing omitted, 68–69; recognizing the same (at the beginning of words), 39–40; sequencing and omitting, 69–70. *See also* Speech sounds
Phonemic awareness, 30
Phonological analysis skills, delay in developing, 134
Phonological awareness, 30; helping children develop, 44; prenatal development of, 126; using literature to stimulate, 31
Phrases, 18; first use of three-word, 131; recognizing the number of words in, 48
Picture cards to build vocabulary and concept, 13
Picture card sound discrimination game, 80
Picture folders, directions for assembling, 139–44
Picture of a designated object, finding a, 14
Pictures: to build vocabulary, 11–12; of city and country, 16; for classification, 12; for contrasts and resemblances, 16; describing and matching objects and, 12; with names that rhyme, 34; noticing similarities and differences in pairs of, 22; from one folder mixed with one from another folder, 15; pairs of, 22; promotion of thought by, 21; with rhyming names, 34; of same object but treated differently, 15; showing sequence of events, 20; of single objects, 23; techniques for presenting, 9; using, 12. *See also* Series of pictures
Picture stories, 20
Pointing to objects, left and right, 115
Prepositions activity, 19
Prepositional phrases, 18
Prepositions, 17–18, 140
Pronunciation of sounds: observing lips, tongue, and teeth during, 79; by teacher, 9

Q

Question of the day, 90
Questions, asking (by 3- to 5-year old child), 131. *See also* Interrogative sentences

R

/R/ sound, missing from most languages, 128–29
Reading: as key to opportunities, 1; most common problem related to, 134; nature of, 2; oral language and, 2
Reading difficulties, early warning signs of, 134
Reading readiness: age for, 133; assessing, 133–34; indications of, 74; tests for, 3, 7
Reading success, prerequisites for, 133

Recalling: a series of directions, 28; words associated with a topic word, 28–29
Recalling activities (examples), 95
Recognition of sound units: phonemes, 30; syllables in student names, 51; syllables in words, 49–51; words in phrases, 48; words in sentences, 49
Recognizing omitted sound units (syllables) from words, 59–60
Relation words (prepositions), 17–18, 140
Relative position, words to describe, 112
Remembering things in sequence, 116
Remembering a word, 27–28
Repeating and passing on a word, 27
Retrieving information, 91
Rhyme, visual association and, 34
Rhyming, 31–36
Rhyming games, 35–36
Rhyming practice, 32–33
Rhyming roll call, 35–36
Rhyming words: discriminating, 34–35; listening for, 32–34
Rhythm instruments, moving hands and feet to the beat of, 25
Rhythm patterns: cards to use with, 143, *144*; reading and playing, 26
Rhythms, 24–26
Right and left, words to describe, 112–13
"Roll the Ball" game, 35

S

Secret word guessing game, 45–46
Sentences: irrelevant, 29–30; practice in saying, 9; putting words together in meaningful, 89; recognizing number of words in, 49; use of complete, 7, 90, 96
Sequence and orientation in groups of objects, noticing change in, 101
Sequence of events, picture showing, 20
Sequence game, 116
Sequencing of games and exercises, 9–10
Sequencing problems, children with, 62
Sequential memory of movements, 107
Series of pictures, finding the object that is different in a, 28
Similar words with changing phonemes, 37
Simon says (game), 113; prepositions and, 19
Singular and plural, 19–20, 28, 141
Slingerland Multisensory Approach to Language Arts, 31, 90–91, 103. *See also* Multisensory strategies
Sound of the day, 79
Sound discrimination, 80; individual phonemes and, 38–39
Sounds in a story, listening for specific, 80
Sound sequencing, 61
Sound-symbol association, difficulty with, 134
Sound symbols, 3
Speaking. *See* Oral expression
Speaking early, results of, 131
Speech sounds, 30; ability to distinguish different, 8; imitation of, 129; kinesthetic motor movements needed to produce, 44; words and, 2. *See also* Phonemes
"Spin the Bottle" game, 35; with sounds, 80
Spoken words, ability to recognize and manipulate phonemes in, 30
Stepping left and right, 114–15
Stimulating brain and language development, 125–32
Stimulation, lack of (during development), 122
Stories: discussions to help children interpret, 96; opinions based on, 97; pictures to illustrate incidents in, 20, 141; pictures to use in reproducing, 21–22, 141; recognizing main ideas in, 96; re-enacting, 95; use of finger to point to words while reading, 94; written by children, 94